Christian Nurture in the Nursery Class

by
MAGGIE MAY BURROW
and
MARY EDNA LLOYD

TEACHER'S TEXTBOOK

For Use With Three-Year-Old Children

HENRY M. BULLOCK, *General Editor*

MARY EDNA LLOYD
Editor, Children's Publications

THE GRADED PRESS

NASHVILLE

TEACHING MATERIALS FOR THIS COURSE

For teaching in the Nursery Class for three-year-olds, each teacher should have the following:

Christian Nurture in the Nursery Class, Teacher's Textbook to be used throughout the year.

My Book for Fall (Winter, Spring, Summer), Pupil's Book to be provided each pupil at the beginning of the quarter. For use of parents and child at home.

Nursery Class Pictures. One set for entire year, for use in the nursery class.

My Picture Card, weekly take-home piece in quarterly packages. For guidance of parents in use of *My Book* at home.

Child Guidance in Christian Living, monthly teacher's publication.

Contents

PART TWO

Introduction

As one of the adults whose privilege and responsibility it is to guide the church-school experiences of three-year-olds, you are aware of the joys of your opportunity. The title, "Teacher," is one by which Jesus was known during his earthly life. In assuming responsibility as a teacher in the church school, let us consider Jesus as the teacher. Jesus showed people what God is like. Those who follow in his footsteps should so emulate his way of life and personality that they become channels through which God's love and purposes reach others. Jesus was a skilled teacher, seeking and finding the needs of those about him, and meeting them to the best of his ability. In his teaching, Jesus used everyday events to guide thoughts, feelings, and behavior. As we guide the experiences of young children, we strive to do likewise. But we must constantly remind ourselves of the limited experiences of these children, entrusted to our care.

We may be encouraged as we recall that the Friend of Children was also the friend of the parents and teachers of children. While we strive to learn and practice the finest possible teaching procedures, we do well to keep in mind that true teaching of the Christian faith is largely a matter of sharing our own attitudes, beliefs, and ways of behaving. The teacher of young children must live a vital Christian life. Such a life includes prayer, study of the Bible, "private and public worship of God," and seeking every opportunity to learn better ways of guiding young children. It takes patience, understanding, and love to interpret Christian living to young children who recognize these virtues long before words are understood. Read "For the Teacher's Own Growth," page 227.

Photograph by Patty Chadwell

I

Goals and Purposes for the Nursery Class

CHANGING PATTERNS IN FAMILY LIFE HAVE PRODUCED A NEED FOR a variety of services which the church extends to young children. A rising birth rate, larger families, and suburban living have led to greater need to provide care for young children while families participate in church activities. Fewer young families live near or with older members of their families. Fewer of them have servants than in former years. More and more, where the family goes the young child must go also.

Along with this increased need for providing care for young children, has come a growing realization and understanding that care is not enough for the three-year-old. His physical well-being must be provided for. Health and safety are important. Furthermore, with a better understanding of ways in which children learn and character develops, has come a growing realization that the nursery class in the church school must provide experiences through which this learning and development may take place along lines which lead to normal growth of Christian character.

The growth in nursery school education has deepened the appreciation of parents and teachers for the best in nursery school procedure. With these procedures the church combines fellowship with those who have deep personal experiences in the Christian faith and a knowledge of the basic principles of teaching.

With the increase in the number of young children who attend the church school, and a deep feeling that three-year-olds need guidance as well as care, many churches provide a separate class for three-year-olds during the Sunday church-school hour. This textbook is planned to aid persons who lead such a class in providing the type of experiences through which the basic aims of Christian education for young children may be achieved. It should help parents to understand what the church is trying to do for their children. Many of

7

the activities and materials included are adaptable for home use. Therefore, this book should be made available to parents as well as teachers.

The accompanying books for use by parents and children are: *My Book for Fall; My Book for Winter; My Book for Spring;* and *My Book for Summer. My Picture Card* is a weekly piece to guide the parents in use of the books.

Purposes for the Nursery Class

The nursery class seeks to provide for the youngest members of the church family a happy introduction to the church school, the joy of finding friends there with whom they may play and work and share good times. Some of these are adult friends who are skillful teachers of little children.

The nursery class seeks to provide opportunities for the three-year-olds to learn to share, take turns, and play together. The nursery class leader attempts to find that way of leading little children that will best introduce them to a Christian way of living and playing together and then to interpret it for them.

There must be a homelike atmosphere that will lead to a sense of security and happiness for the child as he finds himself for the first time in a larger world. When there is such an introduction, as the years go by he will gradually learn to think of the world as given by God to man for a home.

The nursery class leader will try to interpret religiously everything that comes into the life of each child in her group. This religious interpretation will be in the light of the teachings of Jesus who placed a little child in the midst. The Master Teacher met the needs of the individuals in his groups. He faced their problems and taught in the light of the questions that troubled them. Nursery leaders must meet the simple everyday needs of the three-year-olds in their groups if they would adequately minister to these young children. The child is in the midst. The leader will be watched by him. Her interpretation of Christian living as evidenced by her words, her actions, the way she plays and helps others to play, her relations with individual children and with their parents, her attitude to the natural world and its wonders, will teach religion to the child.

Nursery class work should never be confused with "baby-sitting." Every session in a nursery class should be planned for the religious nurture of the child. He will spend most of the time that he is in the group in informal play. But in this play he will be guided to take his place as one member in a group, learning to live the Christian life as the three-year-old may live it.

Goals for the Nursery Class

1. Beginnings of ability to recognize the word God, and dawning wonder that may reach out toward him at any time.
2. Recognition of the word Jesus and a few ideas about him.
3. Recognition of the Bible as a special Book that tells about God and Jesus.
4. Consciousness of always having been "in" the church and a sense of security there.
5. Beginnings of the joys of fellowship with others.

As we study these goals and think of them in terms of the church-school experience of three-year-olds, we are aware that there are differences of opinion as to how much mention shall be made of God in the nursery class. Some workers feel that no child should be able to remember when he first heard the name of God and was led by adults to begin to connect God with events of life. Because of the limited understanding and experiences of children, it is association with Christlike persons that is of greater value than verbal interpretation of life's experiences in terms of God and his relationships. Verbal interpretation is better left until the children are a few years older.

Each teacher will need to think this through for herself. The contagion of Christian personality is the strongest force for teaching children about religion. Occasionally, when children ask questions, a few simple statements may be made to connect God with the meanings of life.

Stories, songs, prayers, and suggested conversations contained in the Sunday-by-Sunday plans are based upon the idea that even very young children can begin to relate God to life. Since the confusion in children's thinking about God is often due to vocabulary difficulties, statements should be kept simple and of such nature that a literal interpretation will be acceptable. For example, as the teachers attempt to help children realize and feel gratitude for the goodness of God in providing food and shelter for his children, they will avoid such statements as "God gives us our food" or "God gives us our homes." Rather, they will say, "We are glad that it is part of God's plan that we should have food" or "How good it is that God helps people to know how to have homes." God as loving, kind, glad when we talk to him in prayer, and ready to help us are true concepts of God which can be shared with children. Nursery teachers will be careful to avoid giving children ideas of God which must be corrected later. Unlearning is likely to leave scars. An interpretation of God's part in such experiences of life as pain and the weather will be included in some of the messages for adults found in the child's book.

What are the facts and ideas about Jesus which we may share with very young children? In later life, we hope that they will come to know, love, and accept Him as Savior, dedicating themselves to living according to his teachings. Any ideas we share with young children should be true and should provide foundations which can be used later for more mature teaching.

Those who use this course as a background for guiding young children will find that Jesus is presented as a special person. He is a kind and loving friend who told people of God's love. The children will hear that Jesus was once a baby, that his family loved him and cared for him. They may associate this experience of Jesus with their own experiences of parental love and care. Pictures will be used with the children that show Jesus as portrayed by artists who have carefully studied the Bible and the land of Palestine. There are those who think it best to begin with the Christmas story, introducing children to Jesus the baby. Others believe it best to start with the Man, the Friend of children and one who showed people what God is like. Since use of stories and pictures with children does not mean that each child sees, hears, and understands what is presented, it is not assumed that each will receive these ideas in the order in which they are presented. Nor do we plan to have these stories told only a few times at certain times of the year. Rather, these are ongoing ideas, often included in our thinking and activities, repeated until they become an integral part of the child's being.

From one copy of each of the pupils' books, the stories and pictures about Jesus may be clipped and made into a book of stories about Jesus, to be used often with small groups or with individual children. The pictures of Jesus included in the books are included in the set, *Nursery Class Pictures*. These large pictures, or those clipped from the books may be framed and hung on the walls, or mounted and placed on the picture rail, and used to suggest frequent retelling of the stories. While the pictures may be particularly emphasized on some Sundays, they will be available for use at all times and often.

Our concern should be to share a few basic ideas about Jesus and to tell over and over again a few selected stories rather than to give children a great deal of information through many stories about Him.

Since children do not always like the same pictures that adults enjoy and are sometimes confused by certain pictures of Jesus, it is wise to mention characteristics of Jesus when we show a picture. For example: "Here is a picture of Jesus with children. Jesus loved boys and girls" or "Here is a picture of Jesus talking with his friends. He told them about birds and flowers."

The horror of pain and death are not realistic to the very young child. He may "shoot you dead," then ask you to get up so that he can do it again. It is not wise to tell young children of the death and Resurrection of Jesus. If a child hears this story at Easter and is upset by it, understanding adults may say, "Yes, Jesus died. But on Easter his friends are glad that he lived again." Only occasionally will a three-year-old raise this question. In the church school, we will not deliberately attempt to share this part of the story of His life with nursery children. Further consideration of the meaning of Easter will be introduced as the child matures and is able to comprehend.

Likewise, we will not emphasize the miraculous aspects of Jesus' birth. The birth of a baby, the love and care of the adults in his family, and the joyous songs are wonder enough for three-year-olds. While this story will naturally be a part of the Christmas activities, it is equally as interesting to three-year-olds at other times of the year.

Although formal worship centers do not have a place in the nursery class, there will be at least one place of special beauty. There should be several spots where things which are beautiful and interesting may be made a part of the conversation and experience. Most teachers like to include an attractive Bible in some place where it is accessible to children. One of the pictures of Jesus, from the lesson material, may be mounted and placed beside the Bible. One of the pictures may be clipped from one of the books or from *My Picture Card* and laid inside the Bible.

The Bible may be referred to as the Book which has in it the stories about Jesus. If children mishandle it, or decide to use it for an extra block in a construction project, the teachers should explain that we take care of all of our books and extra care of this one since it is our special book that tells about Jesus. Avoid use of such terms as "Holy" or "The Word of God" since interpretation of them is difficult in terms understandable to three-year-olds.

Care should be exercised in selection of picture and storybooks based on the Bible. Some of these are unsuitable in content. Others have pictures that repel rather than attract young children. Books recommended for use in the nursery class are frequently listed in *Child Guidance in Christian Living*.

Even before he begins to attend, the young child recognizes the church building and begins to claim it as his own. The possessive pronouns come naturally to him. He should come to feel that the church is "My Church" and the nursery classroom "My room." Care should be taken that the experiences he shares there are happy. During his year in the nursery class, the child may come to know other parts of the church—the playground, the lovely lawn, shrubs and flowers if there are these; the classrooms for older boys and girls and adults; the sanctuary; the kitchen; and (if it is not too gloomy and forbidding) the furnace room. Principle emphasis, however, will be on the nursery classroom and playground space which are provided for him, and upon the happy times he has there with grown-up friends and those his own age.

A secure sense of belonging is a vital part of one's relationship to his church. Like concepts of God, of Jesus, and of the Bible, those shared with three-year-olds should be worthwhile as foundations for continued growing experiences.

Of great value as beginning religious experiences, are the opportunities which the nursery class provides for association with adult Christians who are interested in helping young children to develop happily in the church school. Association with other children his own age is also an opportunity for beginning to realize the rich values of the Christian fellowship. While there is emphasis upon such things as taking turns and sharing, this should not be too strenuously demanded, as self-discovery and the joys of "togetherness" precede the real joy of sharing.

Areas of Religious Guidance

Before considering the setup and procedures through which nursery leaders try to achieve these purposes, it may be helpful to consider the areas of religious guidance around which the year's work is organized. These are listed under six main divisions:

A SENSE OF SECURITY

Security is a basic need of childhood. The nursery class seeks to help a child gain such a feeling, not only in the church school but in his everyday life. Stories and activities planned to contribute to this are built around happy times at church, family life, play, friendly contacts with community helpers and church friends, and enjoyment of nighttime, wind, rain, and changes of season. The association of these realities with God are the basic foundations for spiritual growth.

INSIGHT INTO FAMILY LIFE

This is developed through stories, songs, pictures, and activities of families having happy times working and playing together; of children helping fathers, mothers, and babies; fun at bedtime; grace at meals; family fun at such special times as Christmas and birthdays; fun with older and younger brothers and sisters; and welcoming guests.

DEVELOPMENT OF SELF-RELIANCE

It is hoped that during the year in the nursery class, the child will grow in independence in removing his wraps, playing happily with others, use of big muscle play equipment and art material, putting away toys, and caring for himself at home.

SENSORY EXPERIENCES

The child's eager quest for experience through his senses is sharpened through times when he rakes leaves and enjoys their color and rustling sound; feels bulbs; eats good food; wraps Christmas packages; runs in the wind; drinks good cool water; watches the Christmas candle burn; smells pine or flowers; looks at flowers or bugs through a magnifying glass; listens to music which suggests quiet or rhythmic motion; sings; relaxes during the rest period; splashes in water; plays in the snow; goes for a walk to look for beautiful things. All of these sensory experiences and their interpretation form a foundation of philosophy of life that is Christian.

PLEASURES OF GROUP LIFE

The nursery leader recognizes that the education of three-year-old children depends largely upon the contact between the leader and the child and between the children in the group. All the time the child is in the group he is learning to like or dislike the persons with whom he comes in contact and to enjoy or fear the situations in which he finds himself. All ongoing experiences in his home and church will contribute to his religious growth. This point of view is fundamental to all work with nursery class children.

The child's joy in group life is established and deepened as he comes to recognize adults and other children as his church friends. He learns to enjoy working and playing with them as he sings, enjoys a party, begins to take turns, and puts away toys. These are the beginning steps in church fellowship.

MOMENTS OF WORSHIP

There are no planned worship services in the nursery class. Many opportunities should arise, though, for teachers to worship, and often these may be shared with the children. There will be times when teachers will feel gratitude to God for the privilege of sharing in children's growth and development, especially when such is evidenced in the behavior of the children. There will be other times when the calming effect of the unuttered prayer of a teacher will enable her to act with greater wisdom and kindness in dealing with difficult situations which arise. There will be times when children are filled with joy and wonder, when no words will be spoken at all. All of these contain elements of worship.

There will be times when teachers will use words, prayers, songs, and stories to help children interpret their experiences and feelings in relationship to God and his love. Some of these will be sensory experiences, others related to family life, play, or happy experiences with other children. Teachers may often pray or sing a prayer in the hearing of children. Occasionally, children may be asked to join in. Some Sundays there will be no spoken prayer in the nursery class. Or, the leaders may find several occasions during the session when there will be a prayer with a small group—as at the doll center or while two or three children build with blocks, or three or four gather at the piano to sing. Rarely, if ever, should all of the children be in one group for a prayer.

Children learn by imitation. To be associated with adults who are "at home in the presence of God," who speak of him naturally and to him freely, is a means of acquiring such rapport themselves. Unfortunately, children often are not aware that the adults about them have these feelings or express them in prayer. Too often, children are taught to "say prayers" for listening adults, with little understanding of them as communion with God. It is little wonder that some of them outgrow the habit of prayer, or must relearn it in later childhood.

There is much overlapping in these centers of religious guidance around which nursery workers will build their program of guidance of experiences.

2

The Three-Year-Old

WHAT IS MOST IMPORTANT IN THE NURSERY ROOM? IS IT SPACE, equipment, toys, curriculum material? No. These are important, but all of them are there because of the children. The three-year-olds are the most important factor in the nursery class. And what is a three-year-old like? He is like himself. Each child is an individual and those who work with young children must never lose sight of this. Materials, equipment, and well-planned sessions have value only as they help the children to live and grow in the best possible manner. Jesus said, "I came that they may have life, and have it abundantly." (John 10:10.) It is our responsibility to see that the nursery class helps the three-year-old to so grow at his level of experience, according to his ability, and in keeping with his limitations.

Although each three-year-old is a distinct individual, there are some characteristics which many of them share. A brief look at some of these may help us better to understand the individual.

Physically he has changed amazingly in the past year. He has increased in size, growing taller. He is secure on his feet. He puts only one foot on each step of the stairs as he goes up and down. His muscular co-ordination has increased greatly. He does not "bear walk," but walks and runs sure-footedly. He jumps with two feet instead of stepping off into the air as a two-year-old is likely to do. He can climb more surely than he used to, and seems to want to climb continuously.

To the adult who looks after him, he seems to be constantly in motion, pushing, pulling, climbing, running, exploring. He is trying out his powers and striving to increase them. Dr. James L. Hymes, Jr., an eminent psychologist says, "The three-year-old is constantly struggling for power." A large portion of this struggle seems to be based on his desire for self-discovery, to see how many blocks he can pile on the wagon, how high he can climb, how tall he can stretch.

This desire to grow big and this seeking for himself may bring him into conflict with other children, other adults, and with his environment. He has difficulty distinguishing between the animate and in-animate. His inability to judge spaces and to know his own powers are frustrating and may cause him to strike the interfering adult or object. One three-year-old could not understand why his wagon would not go

15

through the doorway. The hub was caught on the doorframe. In frustration and seeming anger, he jerked and yanked the wagon.

He also has physical limitations. His muscular co-ordination has not increased to include his small muscles. His drive may exceed his stamina and he will become cross, or fall asleep in the midst of an activity. His appetite may vary from being enormous to being extremely finicky.

In his self-discovery, he also discovers others. He attaches himself to a few other friends. His efforts to become acquainted with them are limited by his lack of social knowledge, so he may shove, push, pinch, or pull hair. He still engages in individual play more than group play, but enjoys playing near other children. This parallel play is gradually replaced by small group activity and is a significant part of his growing and learning in the nursery class. Teachers will begin talking about sharing and taking turns and the nursery child will acquiesce, but in his efforts at self-discovery, these social characteristics will be secondary.

Some three-year-olds are timid and will cling to the adult who brings them to the nursery class. Such children need time to feel at home among the adults, other children, and equipment. It is wise not to make an issue with him about participating, for then he must overcome his decision to refuse as well as his natural hesitancy at entering into strange experiences.

Many three-year-olds are chatterboxes. Their vocabularies, information, and understanding are surprising to adults. Others may be almost entirely silent in the nursery class, but go home and tell all about what occurred. Some have not acquired skill in talking and may be in need of a sympathetic adult who will give them time to express themselves or to ask questions.

The three-year-old may be contented and at home in his world, or he may have problems which make his adjustment difficult. To help him continue to develop happily as he acquires new skills in living or solves the problems which make joyous living difficult for him, the church-school workers need to know and understand his environment. This means that the workers should know each child, his family, his home situation, and be known to him. It also means that each worker should know the social pressures in her community. It is important that she know the principles of development of young children. These will help her to interpret for young parents the growth of their children apart from the "to be expected" patterns established by the neighborhood. One who understands child growth

Photograph by Patty Chadwell

and development knows that every child does not need to attend a through-the-week nursery school. Nor does every child ride a tricycle the day he is three years old.

The Young Child's Environment

What then is the world in which the three-year-old lives? Someone has described it as "a jungle of things and people of giant size in which he clings to the safe anchor of his parent's hand." For many children, living in crowded urban areas, this is, unfortunately, too true. For others we are glad to say there is room in which to grow, space for activity, and help in discovering what the world is all about.

First of all, the young child is part of a family. In some cases he is the center of family life, with his wishes and needs dominating the other members of the group. The dominating child is an unhappy child because he does not have the wisdom, strength, or grace to use the power which has been given to him. Nor is it good for any member of the family to dominate. This is as true when the boss is three as it is when the three-year-old is suppressed and given no opportunity to discover his own abilities and direct his own activities.

When the nursery worker visits in the homes of her pupils she comes to know them in relation to their own backgrounds. Tommy is the second son of a young couple who live in a suburban cottage. Although the house is small, he and his brother have a room in which there are shelves for their playthings. They may play freely without interfering with adult activities in other parts of the house. His brother who is five is good natured, gentle, and enjoys playing with Tommy. There is a nice shady, fenced-in back yard with climbing apparatus. The boys have a dog. The mother's parents live next door, so the two little boys have the freedom of two households and a great deal of adult companionship and attention. A number of other young families, with children the age of these two, live near by, and there is much visiting back and forth in the neighborhood. The parents are gentle, fun-loving, but firm in maintaining routine habits of eating, sleeping, and so on. It is little wonder that Tommy entered the nursery class group with ease, took his place among the other children, and enjoys each session.

Susan also is a second child. She has a baby brother as well. Her family lives in a small apartment and Susan must share living quarters with her older sister. The older child resents it when Susan meddles with her clothes, toys, and other possessions. They quarrel a great deal. Susan has regressed into babyish ways since the little brother arrived. Her father is away from home during nearly all of the daylight hours and her mother, who is tired most of the time, is inconsistent in her efforts to guide and control the youngsters. Susan cried a great deal when she first came to nursery class and is inclined to snatch playthings from other children.

Marianne on the other hand is an only child. Her grandmother lives in the home and there is a full-time servant. The four adults with whom she lives give her a great deal of their time and attention. Marianne is inclined to be bossy and demanding, although she is a loving child, eager for the approval of those around her. She likes other children in the nursery class and is beginning to learn how to play with them, but finds it difficult to accept her role as one of a group rather than the center of attention.

Bill's parents are divorced. He lives with his mother and grand-parents in the home of the grandparents. His mother works during the daytime, and his grandmother takes care of him. She is concerned for his health and safety, fearful lest something happen to him, con-stantly warning him about dogs, automobiles, and other hazards. He needs a great deal of encouragement in use of big muscle equipment at the church school and guidance in learning to work and play with other children.

On and on we might go with these sketches of the children who come to our nursery classes, recognizing that while each of them is a part of some family group, each family group, like each child, is different. This calls for different types of help from the church school for the family as well as for the child. Each child has some family background and in each family there are values and difficulties. The values he needs help in appreciating and supporting. The difficulties may be helped by the church school through sharing and counseling, or the child may be guided in making adjustments to them. The church school may provide a brief time of escape from the difficulties and an opportunity to develop in a situation which is planned for him and to meet his needs.

Young children are strongly affected by their home surroundings and their response to life is greatly dependent upon their environ-ment. If the environment gives too much, the child is likely to be-come dependent upon it. If it demands mature behavior of him before he is mature in mind and body, he is likely to be defeated, frustrated, or rebellious in his efforts to meet the demands.

It is important that the church-school nursery teachers know about the child's home background in order that they may try to supple-ment and enrich the desirable phases of it and compensate to the child for some of those aspects which make life difficult for him. To under-stand even slightly the causes of a child's reactions, gives the sympa-thetic adult a clue for guiding his or her responses to the child. There is danger in jumping to conclusions based on superficial knowledge. If the members of his own family who live with him and love him do not always understand him, it is not to be expected that the nursery worker who sees him only occasionally in somewhat artificial circum-stances should do so.

The church-school worker will, however, have a more objective understanding and approach than is likely to be achieved by the family.

The best service the church can render to the child is to help his parents, who are his real teachers. The nursery teacher must never permit himself to be critical or unsympathetic toward parents. They, too, need understanding. The church-school worker whose genuine interest in their child is obvious, and whose understanding of children is undergirded by a serene Christian faith, may well become a family friend whose suggestions are sought and welcomed. In discussions with other workers, each one is wise to avoid any attitude which is unsympathetic and critical. Certainly, discussions of children's problems should be considered confidential.

The Young Child and His Neighborhood

Whether he lives in the open country, a suburban community, or an apartment in the heart of a city, the young child is part of a neighborhood and comes to know some of its customs and people.

The child in the suburban neighborhood is likely to know families much like his own. There may be visiting back and forth to play in the yards and houses of other children. He is likely to come to know others older and younger than himself and to learn to adjust to them. He also comes to know the people who serve the community as mail is delivered, food is purchased, garbage collected, and trips are made to school, church, library, and other community institutions. The child should be helped to develop attitudes of friendly appreciation toward the people who serve him in all aspects of his daily life.

In a city situation, the child who lives in an apartment house will also come to know those who help make his daily life comfortable, the postman, the policeman, delivery boys, and those who work in the apartment house. Here, too, he will have neighbors who may become his friends though his life is more restricted than that of the child in a suburban area.

Teachers need to know not only the type of neighborhood in which each child lives, but also the attitudes which are being taught him. In an effort to protect their children from danger, some parents instill fear and mistrust. While aiding them in their efforts to help the child learn to take care of himself, the teachers have also an opportunity to strengthen the family's efforts to help the child learn to appreciate those who work to make life good for him.

The Young Child and His Church

For many young children, the church is the first social group outside his home and immediate neighborhood of which he comes to feel himself a part. Adults in his home and the nursery class teachers should help him to learn to be glad for the church, to rejoice that it provides a place for him where he may play happily and make friends with adults and other children.

Some children may find it difficult to accept the friendships offered by the church. For a few Sundays it may be wise for the person who brings a child to the class to sit quietly and watch while he gets acquainted and comes to know the people and the procedures there. Some parents may be reluctant to leave their children. This may be due to a fear that the child may cause trouble for adults. Such parents need the reassurance that comes from knowing that teachers feel it a privilege to be of service to young children. Other parents may be unwilling to allow the child to become independent. They may need help in seeing that as long as an adult member of his own family is present, the child is unlikely to develop a good relationship with his teacher. When he is left with the teachers and children in the nursery class, he is likely to turn to the teacher as the mothering person upon whom he can depend for help and guidance.

If he is not urged to participate before he is ready, the child is likely to be attracted by the toys, the activities of the other children, and to enter into the activities. He may be invited to play with the toys and share activities. Otherwise, he may not be aware that this is permitted.

Through songs, pictures, conversation, stories, and simple prayers, the three-year-old will gradually begin to associate his happy church experiences with God. This will perhaps bring into focus the feeling which he should acquire through association, that the church cares for him, that it has prepared for his coming, and that it provides for him. Nursery class leaders will share this idea with children through their manner of living. The joy of Christian fellowship which comes from a happy church relationship is "caught" and this is particularly true in the nursery class.

3

Some Special Problems

THREE-YEAR-OLDS ARE INDIVIDUALS. SOMEONE HAS CLASSIFIED THE age of three as the last stand of rugged individualism in modern life. Being different from others creates problems for the individual as well as for those who seek to help him learn to live happily with others. He needs to preserve the dignity of his own personality and achieve his best development. There are several kinds of individual reaction to life's situation that call for thought and care on the part of adults who work with young children.

The Shy Child

The shy child may be merely deliberate. He may prefer to look, to consider, and to understand what is going on and what is expected of him before he becomes an active participant. Being urged to participate may confuse or irritate him. It may result in a fixed determination not to participate. He is then handicapped by the necessity for overcoming this determination before he can take his place happily with a group. Or, he may be one who has not yet matured beyond the point of preferring parallel play, with others near, rather than group play. It is a mistake to hurry him. Each child should be permitted to mature at his own tempo.

Some shy children are afraid. This may be because they have met with rebuffs or disappointments, even with physical hurt when they have attempted to play with other children. Such children need encouragement.

Or, the child may lack self-confidence. If he has failed, or if more has been demanded of him than he is ready to deliver in the way of social participation, he may be fearful of repetition of such experience. In such a case, he may need the reassurance, not only of a cordial invitation to try out some new activity, but the reward of success. Ronnie was such a child. Overshadowed by larger, older, more active brothers in his home and children in the neighborhood, he had acquired the habit of whining, refusing to try new things, saying, "I can't," and then waiting to be urged. Yet the interest with which he watched as others climbed ladders, played on the slide, or built with the big blocks, revealed a desire to be a part of the general activity.

22

One day as he watched while a group of children marched about on a road they had built, the teacher caught him by the hand and began to sing: "Ronnie walks down the road, Ronnie walks down the road, Ronnie has a lot of fun walking down the road." Slowly, he went along with her, holding her hand. After a few turns around, she handed him a large block and said: "It would be more fun if the road were a little longer." Hesitantly he placed the block at the end of the road. Catching the teacher's hand, they walked along together, the teacher singing again. At the end, she said to the other children, "Our road is better since Ronnie made it longer."

By such simple encouragement and praise, the boy was gradually led to feel that he could share and contribute something which made play better. He never showed signs of aggressiveness in the nursery class, but he gradually changed from watching to doing, and seemed happier.

Mary Lee would occasionally play with a floor toy or hold a doll which was given to her, but would leave any toy and scurry off to sit alone if an adult approached her or said a word to her. The teachers decided to avoid urging her with words. Occasionally, one of them would place a toy near her and quickly go away. Sometimes they would ask another child to take or give something to Mary Lee. She seemed less reluctant to accept the advances of children than of adults. One of the workers visited in her home and so became acquainted with the other members of her family and saw her toys. She suggested that Mary Lee bring Melissa, her favorite doll, to the class to show to the other children.

On the following Sunday, after one or two children had admired Melissa, she was put to bed in the doll bed. Mary Lee looked upset when another child picked her up. A teacher said, "Aren't you glad that Anne likes Melissa, too?" After a few moments, the teacher said, "Anne, Melissa is Mary Lee's little girl. She wants to hold her." Clutching her own doll for a few moments, Mary Lee looked a bit puzzled, then put her back in the bed and told her, "If you get tired of this, Melissa, Anne will rock you." She then turned and began to iron doll clothes. She attached herself to the teacher who had visited in her home, seeming to feel that here was a special friend. Gradually, she began to enjoy the other children.

Teachers will seek to discover the feelings behind the shy child's hesitancy to participate in group activity and try to reassure each at the point of his own need.

The Aggressive Child

The aggressive child may be noisy, may interfere with other children's peaceful pursuit of interests, and may often do things that demand adult attention. He is also likely to be the responsive leader of the group. In this capacity he may become domineering, and may demand that others conform to his wishes. When his efforts are not successful, he may exhibit temper or even tears. Just as is the case with the shy child, the emotional background for the aggressive child may vary.

Learning about his home situation may reveal that he is held down and bossed at home by older children, and the church nursery class may be his opportunity to let off the steam which he has stored up. Or, he may be permitted and encouraged to dominate every situation of which he is a part at home, and his behavior away from home may be a continuation of that.

He may simply have a large supply of physical energy, good health, a bright mind, an outgoing personality, and need help in knowing how to work and play as a part of a group. In our efforts to keep him quiet for the sake of others, and to make him conform, we may seem to nag at this youngster. Certainly, we would be unwise to suppress the instincts of leadership. Such a child is usually of sunny disposition and quick to forgive us, so if we must calm him down often, we can reassure him quickly with a smile and a word of praise when he has done something worthwhile. This is the child who is likely to initiate interesting activities in which others may be encouraged to join. Often he needs help in learning willingness to let a slower, less aggressive child participate fully. He may need encouragement in learning to complete what he begins and in doing things well. The imagination and energy of the aggressive boy or girl need direction. Teachers are challenged to provide this direction with sympathetic understanding.

The Child Who Has Tantrums

The child who has tantrums has probably learned by experience that this is a successful means of getting his own way. This piece of misinformation must be unlearned in order that he may discover better ways of living with others. Adults sometimes give in to the boy or girl who has tantrums in order to avoid embarrassing scenes. The bright child is likely to repeat a way of behaving which has been successful in securing for him something he wants. Most students of child behavior are in agreement that wholesome letting alone and being sure that such behavior never proves profitable, is the best means of eliminating tantrums.

If a child has a tantrum in the nursery classroom, it may be necessary to pick him up and take him outside to prevent his upsetting other children. Weeping is highly contagious. The important thing is that the adults involved shall maintain their own calm sense of balance. After all, an adult who loses his temper can do little to help a child control his. Almost any child is likely to have a few tantrums during the ages of two to four. It is the frequent sufferer with whom we are concerned.

Apparently trivial things can cause temper tantrums. The spark which sets off the blaze is not the real cause, it is some inner dissatisfaction which literally boils over. It may be due to having too much adult supervision and being hedged in with too many "noes." It may come from not having enough rules to which he knows he must submit. Young children need the sense of security which comes from a realization of authority! Due to the inconsistency of adults in their relationships with children, both of these sometimes happen to the same child. Wise adults will try to think through the possible causes of confusion and dissatisfaction which may exist in the child's life and correct them. This is a home responsibility. The church-school teacher may help by pointing out the various possible causes of tantrums with the suggestion that the adults responsible for his everyday care and guidance work out a policy of helping the child to overcome them. A child may be frightened into swallowing his rage but the effect on his personality is likely to be seriously harmful.

In addition to removing him from the group and leaving him alone as nearly as possible, the nursery class workers need to be very careful to help the child regain a sense of acceptance as quickly as possible when the storm has subsided. One little boy after the birth of a baby sister frequently had tantrums in the class for three-year-olds. At home, he seemed happy about the baby, but after a few moments in the class he would begin to throw toys about, to fight other children, finally flinging himself upon the floor, beating his head and yelling. A motherly worker would pick him up and take him to a rest room where she would sit nearby while he cried it out. There was a rocking chair in the room. One morning, after washing his face and talking to him quietly, she sat down and took him into her lap and began to rock. He snuggled close to her and she asked him, "Do you like to be rocked?" "Yes," the little boy answered. Then after a pause, he added, "I like to be rocked." This suggested to the leader that the child had not been rocked since the baby came. A visit with the parents confirmed this suspicion. As long as he was secure in his mother's nearness at home, he did not mind this, but when he was insecure, away from her, it represented a deprivation. When his father began rocking him at bedtime and his mother occasionally held him on her lap for a few moments each day, the tantrums disappeared. Soon he was able to be happy away from his home, as well as at home.

Mary Jane's parents were so proud of their beautiful daughter that, without meaning to do so, they had permitted her to become the mistress of their home and to dominate both of them. For fear of making her unhappy they attempted to let her make many decisions for which she was unready. Consequently, she had become unsure of herself and did not remain satisfied long with any choice. Her habits were uncertain as to bedtime, eating, and toileting. When she entered the nursery class she was at first surprised, then resentful to discover that toys and equipment belonged to all children. She could not expect that things be given to her upon demand. Other children sometimes claimed the teacher's attention. After a few sessions, Mary Jane began flinging herself upon the floor and screaming when things did not please her. When she was permitted to cry it out, one of the workers who understood that she needed sympathy and a sense of being loved said to her, "I sometimes feel ugly inside, too. I have found that doing something very hard helps me to feel better." Mary Jane was given a mallet and a knock-out bench. She pounded vigorously for a few moments. On another occasion she was guided to tear up sheets of newspaper, wad them up, and kick them about. After awhile this became amusing rather than an outlet for emotions. Once she was able to laugh at her own ugly feelings, they began to disappear. Her parents were helped to see that she was not yet mature enough to decide everything for herself and that she would be happier if some routine regulations governed her life. The nursery class workers were able to help the child through sympathetic effort and to offer suggestions to her parents.

The Child Who Hurts Other Children

The child who hurts other children by biting, hitting, scratching, kicking, or spitting on them, presents a twofold problem. There is need for protecting the rights of other children. There is also need for helping the child himself to learn and practice ways of behaving which will make him socially acceptable. In some instances, such behavior is indicative of a desire to attract attention or to become acquainted with other children. In others it is used as a means of striking out against whatever is near because he feels an inner disturbance. His action has little or no connection with the object of his attack. In fact, such children are likely to kick or strike an inanimate object, such as a chair or a wagon which happens to be in their way. Their attacks on other children are apparently unprovoked. It is the responsibility of adults who guide them, to try to discover the basic cause of resentment as well as to instruct them in more desirable forms of behavior.

In the case of the child who uses these methods to attract attention, or to become acquainted with others, it is suggested that the adult shall stoop or sit down at the eye level of the child and take both his hands in hers in order to be sure of his attention. She may then state calmly and forcefully, "We keep our hands to ourselves or use them to help other children. We help others when we give a ball or other toys. We use our hands in the right way when we build with blocks or put puzzles together." Avoid negative statements. One psychologist goes so far as to say that the young child does not hear the "Don't" in such statements as, "Don't pinch the baby," "Don't hit your playmate," and that repetition of the description of the offense helps the child remember it and thus makes it more likely to be repeated. We are aware that we help children most when we point out to them good ways of living.

Sometimes a child's hurting of others goes to the point where he must be removed from the group and told that he may return when he is ready to play happily with others.

If the behavior comes from some basic, inner dissatisfaction with life, the church school can do little more than help parents recognize the situation and urge that they discover and correct the source of the child's upset condition.

Whether the case be one in which a child is just trying to learn how to get along with others and by trial and error method adopts some procedures which are not acceptable, or whether his problem is deep seated, teachers and parents should recognize that he needs help and should work together to provide it. Whatever the reason for unsocial behavior, teachers must learn to protect other children from attack.

When one child hurts another, comfort should be offered and the hurt child assured that the teachers are very sorry. To force the offender to say that he is sorry is likely to be causing him to be insincere and to add falsehood to the other offense.

"I'm sorry," was Doug's remark each time he pinched another child. The brief apology was usually stated with such complete sincerity that it was usually accepted by the teacher who then sought to console the pinched child, but let Doug run off to play. Within a few minutes, another child would burst into loud screaming or would double over in pain, not making an outcry, but with tears streaming down his face. Doug might be nearby looking with apparent concern, or he might be far across the room, joining another child in play. It was after about three sessions of these outbursts that the teachers discovered that Doug "pinched and ran," or "pinched and apologized," but that his favorite and sure way of securing what he wanted from another child was a hard pinch.

Almost all of the good books on child study provide help for each of these areas of misbehavior. Teachers and parents should read several references in each case and between them work out a way of helping the child, seeking professional advice if it is needed.

Children Who Are Leaders

Educators say that our society fails to develop to the fullest the natural abilities of our most gifted children and that we are so busy trying to get everyone to conform that we fail to develop fully the abilities of our leaders. While we certainly do not wish to make a child conceited by giving the bright, aggressive child more than his share of praise and recognition, neither should we be guilty of holding him back. Such children are quick to respond to suggestions and often guide other children to happier experiences. In a laboratory school, Jerry seized upon the small travel bags, directed several others to pack for a vacation, escorted them to the rocking boat and waving happily to all around shouted, "We are going for a vacation." He and several others had a very happy experience which led from the boat trip to a visit in the housekeeping center and on to a listening experience at the record player. Here again it was Jerry, who listening attentively to the record about the church from the *My Book Album*, asked that the part about the bells ringing be played over and over. Because of his joyous responses and inventiveness, other children followed him eagerly.

Photograph by Michael Graf, Jr.

On the other hand, Tommy, who was equally as well developed mentally, wanted to boss every detail of the construction of a road and building with big blocks. He yelled and hit others when they moved a block, even a little bit. When a teacher intervened, he left the group and sulked alone. Over and over he was told, "You think of good things to do, and so does Mary Jane. In nursery class we learn to work together." Over a period of weeks he began to show some improvement and it is obvious that the nursery class will be helpful to him in overcoming the obstacles to development of his natural capacities for leadership.

Care should be taken that the child who is a natural leader shall be given opportunities to learn to work happily with other children so that his abilities are utilized and his talent for leadership encouraged. At the same time, workers will be careful to help less aggressive children have an opportunity to see that their ideas are enjoyed and appreciated by the group, and that the dominant child does not become overly aggressive.

Working with young children requires a great deal of careful observation, tactful guidance, and evaluation in order that children may help one another as they learn to work and play together. Since the church nursery class is often the first social group outside his own family to which a child belongs, it has a fine opportunity to be helpful at this point. Teachers need to keep in mind that children have to learn to live with others, they do not know this instinctively.

Special Situations

Sometimes events which occur in the life of a child affect his responses to others and create difficulties for him. A severe illness may be followed by regressive, babyish behavior. Time and help will be needed to regain social progress. Sometimes, this regression may follow the birth of another child in his home, or the serious illness of one of his parents. Any event which upsets or changes his routine should be watched for possible effects on his emotional reactions.

When illness, his own or that of someone else in his family, causes him to revert to babyish ways he should be treated with patience, given a little more loving attention, and encouraged to regain his lost ground.

When families move into new homes in the same community or to new communities, young children sometimes feel that they have lost their homes. Some of them have been known to cry to be taken home. When a family is to move, the child should be prepared for this. If the new home is being built, he should visit the site of the new building, learn where his room is to be, where his favorite toy is to be kept, what the advantages are of the new situation, and be prepared for making the experience a happy one. If the move is to a new community, his family should be encouraged to take time to help him discover his place in the new community. They will help him get acquainted with new playmates, his new play space, and how he may get in the house quickly. This may mean delay in the physical aspects of getting settled in the new home but will be worthwhile.

When the move involves entrance into a new church-school group, one of the workers should visit the child in his home, getting acquainted with him and his family in his own environment and assuring him of a familiar person to greet him when he comes to the class. Emotional attitudes are easily shared. His family should be careful to speak happily of differences in the new situation and the old, and to reassure him as much as possible. Finding places to keep and use familiar possessions will help him feel at home in the new setting. The recognition of books and pictures and of familiar procedure will be helpful.

It is important that the three-year-old be prepared as much as possible for changes in his way of living, that he be helped to look forward to the good features of the change, and that he be reassured by feeling that he shares the experience with the rest of the family.

Some changes create difficult adjustments for every member of the family, such as those brought about by tragic accidents or death. Here, the attitude of the older persons whom the child loves and trusts is likely to be shared by him. If we are to share a beautiful Christian philosophy with our children it is necessary that we have and live by such a philosophy. It is natural that we shall be shocked by tragedy and grieved by the loss of those we love. But, if ours is a serene Christian faith, firmly established in the assurance of God's love for us and his interest in us, and looking forward to eternal life, no tragedy or loss will destroy it. There are those who believe it wise to keep any knowledge of trouble, grief, or death away from young children. This is almost impossible and may lead a child to feel that he is being excluded by his family. While he should be spared the heavy weight of a family's burden as much as possible, he should not be allowed to feel shut out.

Adults may be helped to gain control of their emotions in their effort to protect children, since it is natural for a child to become bewildered and upset when the adults, to whom he is accustomed to look for reassurance, go to pieces. The three-year-old cannot understand death, but he can understand that the adults in his family love him, love one another, and love God, and that they remain loving, even in times of trouble. Through numerous experiences with plants, pets, and other forms of life, children may begin to recognize death as an ongoing part of living. As they grow older, they may begin to formulate their own philosophy of immortality. For the very young child, the realization that he is part of a family unit in which there is love, even in time of pain and trouble, is a good foundation upon which to build such a philosophy in later life.

4

The Nursery Class Teacher

THE CHURCH NURSERY CLASS SHOULD COMBINE THE BEST OF
nursery school practices with the best in Christian education. This
does not mean that only trained nursery workers should teach three-
year-olds in the church school. It does mean that Christian men and
women who work with this group should be persons who will combine a love of young children with a willingness to learn desirable ways
of guiding their growth and development.

This teaching material is designed for such workers. It presupposes
that the nursery class worker has a genuine, growing Christian experience, a love for and desire to serve young children, and a willingness to follow accepted nursery class procedures.

Few churches would be able to staff their nursery groups with
professionally trained workers. Most churches will use men and
women who wish to be of service to children and to the church. As
such workers study and grow, they will discover that teaching material is a starting point, not a fixed set of rules for procedure. For
the inexperienced teacher, however, it is wise to follow the materials
carefully, trying to understand the basic, underlying principles of
religious education and gradually developing flexibility and resource-
fulness.

Nursery class workers should be healthy, cheerful, pleasant persons. They should not be effusive or affected in their relationship with
children. While there are genuine bonds of affection between teachers
and children, maudlin sentimentality has no place.

One worker says that she has discovered that it is wise not to
touch a child until that child has voluntarily touched her. A shy child
or one who withholds himself from the group may need a reassuring
physical contact, possibly a gentle pat on the shoulder.

Expressions of courteous appreciation and approval are more
acceptable to young children than assurances of affection. By smiles,
voice, and manner, the adult who teaches him assures the young child
of approval and friendship.

Since service in the nursery class is varied, the personalities and
talents of nursery workers may also vary. In order to serve as leading
teacher of the group, the worker should be willing to devote time to
planning, to guiding the work of those who assist, and to coming to

know the children in their homes and counseling with their parents. The leading teacher should be capable of carrying out the plans outlined in the curriculum material. She must be open-minded and eager to acquire knowledge and understanding about child development and nursery procedures.

Helping teachers should have these same characteristics. Sometimes a helping teacher who is often a man, is the mothering (or fathering) person whose greatest contribution may be in home contacts and in helping the homesick child to become adjusted to the church-school situation. Another helping teacher may keep records, or if a skilled

Photograph by Minrod

musician, render such special service as playing the piano. All workers should recognize themselves as teachers, studying the materials, working with the children, and sharing in planning and evaluating in order to improve their experiences as teachers.

The education of young children is not solely a feminine responsibility. The role of the father is changing in our society. He shares equally with the mother the responsibility of caring for and loving the children. Children like and enjoy associations with men. Men often find that working in the nursery class is a worthwhile church service. Frequently a husband-and-wife team finds service in the nursery class very rewarding. Even grandparents have been known to make a fine contribution.

It is presupposed that the nursery class leaders are Christian persons, for Christianity is caught by these younger children; it is not taught them verbally. Since the church school is a school of religion, nursery class workers should have growing religious experiences that make of them people worthy of imitation by the children. There are and will continue to be differences of opinion as to the extent to which nursery class teachers should seek to express in words to three-year-olds ideas about God, Jesus, the Bible and other phases of religion. Certainly, no worker should say what he has not experienced as true in his own life. Children are quick to detect insincerity in any form.

On the other hand, there are those Christians to whom speaking normally and naturally of God's part in human life is as natural as breathing. Such persons will, naturally, speak of God to children. The difficulty which these teachers will need to overcome is that of staying within the range of the young child's vocabulary, understanding, and experience in order that they may not confuse him or give him wrong ideas which he will have to unlearn later. Throughout this material, suggestions are given as to how this may be done. It is hoped that it will enrich the ability of the inarticulate and serve as a guide to those to whom talking of religion is easy and natural. Throughout its use, however, we will keep in mind that children learn primarily through their own experiences, through the things they see, do, smell, feel, and hear, and especially through their relationship with other persons. Living in an atmosphere which is dominated by the principles of Christ and being guided by adults who live according to his teachings will provide better learning than the most carefully planned verbal expressions.

Since young children become attached to the persons they know, it is important that nursery class workers shall be regular and prompt in their attendance. In situations where children stay for care during the church worship services, it is important that good teaching procedures are continued. At least one of the nursery class workers should stay during the church worship service. The program may be varied somewhat for the extended time, but the atmosphere is likely to be less changed if one of the workers is familiar with the nursery class procedure.

Nursery class teachers should be on hand to greet the children when they arrive. The teachers' wraps, hats, and purses should be put away in an inconspicuous place. The teachers should be relaxed, ready to help children feel at home when they come. This will add to the security of the children. One child seeing a teacher on the street said with pleasure, "Look, Mother, there's the lady who lives at the nursery class." In some churches one or more workers are better able to come early than are others, hence they take this responsibility. They attend to the last minute preparation of the room, ventilation, and supplies.

In order really to share the activities of children, adults who work with them should dress comfortably in clothing which will enable them to move about freely and to sit on the floor. No worker should ever wear a hat during the session since this gives the children a feeling that she is ready to go away and leave them. Somberness and over-dressing are both to be avoided.

Teachers should continually strive to improve their services to children. This will come through enriched personal life, achieved through prayer, Bible reading, and study. Since the worker with children relinquishes the privileges of sharing in an adult church-school class, she should avail herself of other opportunities. These may include sharing the adult worship and study which is made possible by participation in communal worship service, evening study groups, and special courses for personal enrichment.

The church library should afford a number of guides for personal enrichment and study as well as books on child development, ways of teaching young children, and in the general field of Christian education. Institutes, leadership schools, and other workers' meetings should be shared by nursery workers. Participation in a laboratory school often leads to enthusiastic new approaches.

Regular study and preparation for Sunday-by-Sunday sessions are important. Not just the leading teacher, but all who work with three-year-olds should study the teachers' and pupils' materials. Specific suggestions are included each month in the magazine, *Child Guidance in Christian Living,* in addition to many other interesting articles concerning the Christian education of children. Workers should plan together, comparing ideas concerning individual children, activities, and class sessions.

Teachers in the nursery class are not baby sitters. They are privileged to share and guide the growth and development of young children during an important year of childhood. In order to do this they should seek all possible means of improving their service, teaching out of the abundance of riches of mind and spirit.

Bible Study for Teachers

One of the sacrifices made by adults who teach very young children in the church school, is to give up the privilege of sharing in the activities and study of an adult church-school class. This sometimes leads such workers to feel that they are missing the guidance they need for Bible study on an adult level.

A study of material prepared for children and the joys of sharing the growth and development of children is ample compensation for the sacrifice; but wise nursery workers will endeavor to fill in the gap in their adult level experience through Bible study, alone and with others. This may be done in a variety of ways. A personal study, based on the lesson materials for adults will be helpful. There are special units, such as the Basic Christian Books, *Know Your Bible* Series, *Know Your Faith* Series, and others available from The Methodist Publishing House serving you. Lists of these are published in the adult publications of the church school from time to time.

Studying alone is more profitable if supplemented by group study, and as most children's workers have the same need, some children's workers have organized groups for Bible study. They meet at some hour other than the Sunday morning church-school hour when they are busy working with children. Such groups may meet one afternoon or evening a week for special set periods of study, or throughout the year. In some cases, they have sought the leadership of a person who teaches an adult Bible class on Sunday morning and have found that person glad to lead their group.

In addition to Bible study classes, it is important that those who work with young children shall avail themselves of opportunities for sharing worship with other adults and participating in groups who discuss current affairs in the light of religious principles.

Some such groups meet as part of the Sunday Evening Adult Fellowship. In one such class of parents and teachers, a genuine fellowship and ways of working together developed. If you are interested in setting up such a group, it is well to discuss it fully in your children's division council, then work through the commission on education to be sure that your plans are effective.

Since there is a limited quantity of biblical material used with nursery children, some parents and workers feel dissatisfied, and complain that there is too little Bible in the material. It is not through words or stories or pictures that one teaches the Bible to three-year-olds. It is the life that parents and teachers live that interprets its message in a language understandable to these young children. Thus parents and teachers share out of the abundance of the riches of their own lives.

The following list of suggestions is given in a concise form for easy reference. The nursery class leader will do well to read these suggestions frequently and to check any that she feels she needs to watch especially.

- Have a calm, unhurried procedure.
- Avoid hovering over children or interfering with them, especially when what they are doing is not harmful to others or to themselves.
- Stoop to the level of the child occasionally when speaking to him.
- Minimize bumps and falls. Sympathize, but avoid "babying."
- When questions are answered or an explanation is given, make it simple. Avoid confusion of ideas. Make statements brief and use words within the understanding of the child.
- Always repeat directions in the same way.
- Only one person at a time should give directions.
- Expect desired conduct.
- Watch tone of voice. Keep it pleasantly modulated. Enunciate clearly.
- Smile frequently.
- Avoid talking too much. Listen and learn from the child.
- Cultivate a calm, pleasant emotional attitude.
- Be consistent at all times.
- So far as possible delete the words "hurry" and "don't" from the vocabulary used with three-year-olds.
- Learn to laugh *at* oneself and *with* the children.
- Study to be a growing person.
- BE PATIENT!

5

Parents of Nursery Class Children

NURSERY WORK IS HOME WORK. THE PARENTS ARE THE LITTLE child's first and greatest teachers. The nursery class can only supplement the work of the home. How may parents and teachers work together for the religious nurture of the three-year-old child?

Need for Parent Co-operation

The nursery class needs the parents. The child's family is a part of the child. Family joys, fears, anxieties react on the little child. He senses tense atmosphere. He absorbs security, calmness. The homes from which the children come influence the group that the nursery leader is seeking to guide religiously in this introduction to church life. Nursery class work cannot be carried on apart from parent work.

The parents wish to know how the nursery class leader plans for this first "out-of-the-home" religious nurture of the child. The leader will help the parents and may avoid difficulties for herself if she will have a list of suggestions typed and ready to give parents who come to observe in the nursery class. This list may be called "Hints for Observers." It might include such suggestions as:

> Parents are requested to refrain from conversation with one another when any of the children are playing near them.
>
> Parents are requested to co-operate by not laughing at the children nor at their remarks. If a child talks to a parent, it is to be expected that there may be opportunities to laugh with the child.
>
> When the child enters the nursery classroom the responsibility for his behavior is assumed by the nursery class leader. Parent visitors are requested to co-operate by recognizing the fact that all behavior problems will be handled by the nursery class leader.
>
> When parents expect to visit during the entire session, they are requested to remove their wraps just as the children do.
>
> The leader appreciates the opportunity to discuss with the visitors any procedures including the activities, story or lack of story, the use of prayer, the reason for certain songs.

Such discussion with parents must obviously come *after* the session. It should be done out of the child's hearing.

38

This list may include other suggestions, but these will help the visitors to realize that they are welcome and that the leader has made certain preparations for their co-operation. Pencil and paper should be provided for jotting down questions or comments.

The nursery class will succeed only as there is close co-operation with the home. For example, feelings of worship are expressed more readily and easily when the atmosphere of both home and church are conducive to spontaneous reaching toward God. If the parents and the nursery class both provide opportunities for taking turns, the child more quickly learns that this is an acceptable form of behavior.

Some Ways Parents Help

There are many ways in which parents and nursery class leaders may co-operate for the good of the children. Parents help the nursery class leader by seeking to understand the reasons for certain procedures. They may stop to ask why there was no story or they may ask why the children went outdoors to plant flowers during the session. The leader appreciates this interest on the part of the parents and is glad to explain the reasons. She will point out the religious values in having the little child plant seeds. She speaks of the feel of the earth and the fact that the child experiences something of wonder when he realizes that he may plant the seed but he cannot make it grow. There will be rain and sunshine. Then the leaves come and finally, the flower. The seeds grow. After such an experience there is deeper meaning in the prayer, "Thank you, God, for seeds that grow."

Parents may also co-operate by reading carefully each part of the pupils' material, *My Book for Fall, Winter, Spring, Summer*. The leader will add emphasis value if she points out certain hoped-for results in informal conversation with the parents or through parents' meetings.

One important way for parents to co-operate is by providing name labels for coats, hats, gloves, rubbers, and purses. These may be bought name labels, or inexpensive paper muslin or tape labels on which the child's name has been typed or written.

When parents' meetings are held regularly, parents may take the responsibility for a few moments of social time after the discussion. Parents who contribute from their actual experience help other parents and the leaders immensely. Parent-child problems frequently repeat themselves for other parents with only minor change. Some fathers and mothers of nursery children set aside times for meeting in the nursery classroom. Such an evening provides delightful opportunities for parents to visit together and get acquainted with one another and with the leaders. Fathers may take care of any carpentry work, painting, or repairing that needs to be done. The mothers may wish to paint also or they may be willing to make new doll clothes and curtains, and do necessary laundry. Sometimes these parents decide to make a special offering for the purchase of new equipment. Sometimes a parent will be able to secure such equipment at wholesale price. These are practical ways in which parents and nursery class leaders co-operate for the happiness of the children.

Parents may take turns getting the children in a neighborhood to the nursery class on time. Another phase of parent co-operation is the use of special talents for the religious nurture of the children. A mother who sings very beautifully may be willing to come in to play with the children and then sing some of their well-loved nursery class songs. A doctor father may be willing to bring his stethoscope at the time the children are talking about the doctor friend. He could play doctor with the children. He might bring a small pair of bathroom scales and let the children take turns being weighed. A family with a garden or fish pond may co-operate through inviting the children to visit their yard.

In some churches it may be possible to have a table on which are books, pamphlets, and magazines with articles pertinent to the problems the parents are facing. This table may be in the vestibule, the social room, the room in which the parents meet, or one of the adult classrooms. The nursery class leader may suggest materials for this table. A committee of parents from the nursery class may carry the heaviest part of the responsibility, and at least one parent should be responsible each week for seeing that someone is at the table to check out the material to the parents who wish to borrow. Fathers should be encouraged to have just as great responsibility along this line as mothers.

At Christmas time an exhibit of books and suitable toys for young children may be borrowed from local stores. Parents and the nursery leader may be responsible for such an exhibit. This exhibit should be selected carefully. Unfortunately many commercial toy houses do not consider the educational values of the toys. The nursery class leader will apply the same standards as those used in selection of toys for use in the nursery class. (See pages 54-60.)

Still another way in which parents may co-operate with the nursery class leader is to provide a calm, quiet atmosphere at home from which the child will leave to go to nursery class on Sunday morning. Children who are hurried into a nursery class situation frequently find it most difficult to adjust to other members of the group and the entire session may be spent in helping them to adjust happily. The nursery class leader may be able to think of many other practical ways in which parents and nursery class leaders may cooperate.

When Parents Make Problems

Unfortunately, parents sometimes make real problems for the nursery class leader. There is the parent who brings the child into the group and says, "Now don't cry. Don't cry when I go." Such a parent expects the child to cry and usually he does.

There is the oversolicitous mother. (Sometimes this is the oversolicitous father or grandparent.) This person is anxious that the child shall make a good appearance, shall be equal to the other children in social development, and shall give evidence of being unusually bright. Among the oversolicitious parents is the one who has exceptionally high standards for the child's speech or urges him to be overly polite. Another form of the oversolicitous parent is the mother or father who will not let the child grow up. They coddle him, do everything for him, even tell him what to say, occasionally smother his initiative with their solicitude until he merely sits and lets them think and act for him. Sometimes such a parent is solicitous of a child's health and overcoddles him physically also.

Another parent may overestimate or underestimate the child's ability. Much patience is required to help this parent to understand that the nursery leader is deeply interested in helping the child. Usually it is easier to improve an underestimation of the parent's opinion of a child's ability than to limit an overestimation. The child may not be capable of doing all that is expected of him and the overstrain of trying to meet advanced expectations in the home can cause serious troubles. These troubles may develop into behavior problems or even personality difficulties, such as overaggressiveness, shyness, or inhibitions.

Problems are frequently made when parents hurry the child too much or when there is a lack of understanding. This may be a lack of understanding of the child and his needs or it may be too limited insight of the educational procedure in the nursery class. Again, parents may make it difficult for the child to gain the most from the nursery class when they laughingly joke, or perhaps criticize the leader, the minister, or the church. The tone of voice influences the child's attitude. Long before he can understand the meaning of the words of the parents, he knows the implications of the tone. A most difficult problem arises when the parents decide to leave all religious nurture to the church. Parents should be helped to realize that there can be no adequate religious nurture of little children except as the church and home work together.

Parents' Conferences

Conferences with the nursery class parents usually classify into three types. There are the regular meetings, the occasional meetings, and the individual conferences. Notice of regular or occasional meetings may be tied or pinned to the child's coat on Sunday and so sent home. Notices may be mailed or the leader may telephone to the parents when the child is absent.

The church bulletin is another help in arousing the parents' interest in the nursery class. The church bulletin, a parents' bulletin board, or a special nursery department news bulletin, may carry notices of the regular or occasional meetings for parents of nursery children. The church bulletin may also include short notes regarding any nursery class news that would be of special interest to adult members of the church. Perhaps this would include a report of new equipment or of the freshly painted walls. The church bulletin and a special nursery department bulletin help establish home contacts, and also to make persons who have no other contact with this youngest group in the church school conscious of the work of the nursery class.

REGULAR MEETINGS

For the most part these meetings should take the form of discussion groups rather than of lectures. Discussion helps the parents to feel that they are contributing members of the group. As the nursery class leader, a parent, or a committee of parents guides these discussions they will seek to provide an informal atmosphere in which everyone will be comfortable and will wish to participate. They will raise questions and add comments from their background of experience and preparation. The pooled experiences of the parents will help more retiring members of the group to feel at ease. Often it is a satisfaction when parents find that other fathers and mothers face exactly the same problems that have been worrying them. They realize that their child is not different, that he is not naughty because he reacts in certain ways or does not do just as they think he should, that this is just a normal part of growing older.

Occasionally, these regular meetings are fully organized groups with the presiding officer, secretary, and sometimes a treasurer. The dues from such meetings often help add to the nursery class equipment, or may be used for some philanthropic purpose, or may add books to the parents' library.

These regular meetings may be carried on over a long period of time or they may continue for a few months and then disband to reconvene a few months later. Some nursery groups have regular meetings only four times a year and make one of the meetings a picnic for the teachers, parents, and nursery age children.

OCCASIONAL MEETINGS

In other nursery groups, the plan for a regular meeting has not proved satisfactory. But the parents wish to get together occasionally to discuss some of the questions regarding the work of the nursery class, or just to talk together with someone who knows little children.

INDIVIDUAL CONFERENCES

The most valuable type of conference so far as meeting the need of the individual parent is the one with that parent. Occasionally, the father and mother together will seek an opportunity to confer with the nursery leader. Again, just one parent may talk over some problem or report some happy occasion in the family. Perhaps the leader will do nothing but listen and be sympathetically understanding. Many parents need just such an understanding friend, but it takes much preparation and training for the leader to meet such problems adequately. Although the leader only listens at the time, she needs to know something of psychology that will help interpret for her what underlies the difficulty the parent is facing. She needs to know teaching methods and child development so that she can encourage a parent to realize that his child is developing along lines that are to be expected. This presupposes a knowledge of mental hygiene, physical development, and social growth as well as religious nurture.

Home Contacts in the Nursery Class

As has been previously stated, nursery class work is really home work. The parents and other members of the family and the children in the neighborhood with whom the child plays, the persons with whom he lives and talks and plays all day are the ones who have the greatest influence upon his life. This, then, is a major reason for nursery class leaders to establish home contacts. On the other hand, most parents enjoy and desire the friendly association and informal visits with the nursery class leaders.

Most nursery class leaders are busy persons. Homemakers, or persons employed during the day, give their time and effort as volunteer leaders on Sundays. They have very little time to visit in the homes of the children. When the leader is employed all day and the three-year-old child goes to bed early, an evening call means that the child is not present or that the mother is busy putting him to bed.

Personal visitation is the first thought in "home contact" and yet there are other desirable contacts. It is often possible to find a young mother with the educational viewpoint which fits her for nursery work who is willing to assume the responsibility for visits in the home. Sometimes a parish visitor or a deaconess can render assistance at this point. The nursery home visitor and the nursery class leader should confer with these other visitors frequently so that they may be sure that the purpose and plan of nursery class work is clearly understood. The nursery class leader should make it a point to visit just as often as possible in addition to the help of these home visitors. The nursery class builds on good work done by the nursery home visitor.

The hearty, friendly co-operation of the pastor of the church is another possibility. The nursery leader and the pastor who calls in the home need to work in close sympathy and understanding. Each should stand ready to explain the work of the church and to report to the other any special cases or items of interest.

Notes, letters, and telephone calls also help establish contacts with the home. When a child is absent it takes but a few minutes to make a telephone call, and the parent is delighted that the leader has missed Joan and is calling to inquire about her.

A personal note written to the child who is ill is treasured by him. There are other times than illness when notes are of value. The leader who wrote to Teddy to tell him how glad she was to hear the news that he had a new baby sister endeared herself to the three-year-old and also to the parents and grandparents! When Bryan had a difficult time adjusting to the group and finally made just a slight advance, the leader wrote him a note during the week. She mentioned the fact that she was glad that he had played with them on Sunday and suggested that on the following Sunday she planned to bring a new ball. Perhaps he would enjoy playing ball with Jack and Martha and Ruth. This gave Bryan something to look forward to. The following Sunday he ran in asking, "Where is the new ball?"

When Louise had whooping cough and Marion was quarantined with scarlet fever, notes were written on Sunday evening and mailed to both homes. Some little interesting event of the morning session was told. Occasionally, there was a picture enclosed that held interest for the three-year-old child. These notes were personal greetings. They carried good wishes from the leader to the members of that home.

Birthday notes are also appreciated by the parents and enjoyed by the children. Many leaders prefer to write brief friendly greetings on a small-size correspondence card. This takes a little more time and thought than the commercial cards, but it is more personal. There is one suggestion. When a birthday note is sent, the leader should be sure that it arrives on the birthday and not even one day later. This personal interest in the child is a real home contact.

Sometimes telephone calls are used to tell the mother of the child's advance in social life, or some other evidences that he is growing. When John, after weeks of passively sitting in nursery class watching the other children, suddenly entered into group activities and became one of a small group who enjoyed a game of "Ring Rosy," the leader called John's mother to tell her how happy she was at this evidence of his beginning to be a co-operative member of the group.

Added to the possibilities of visits, notes, and telephone calls, there are "seconds" of individual contact when Mother or Father brings the child to nursery class or comes for him after the session. Just a friendly sentence, a question as to Jane's health after her long siege of illness denotes interest, or perhaps the report that Ned did not seem quite like himself this morning. Had he been emotionally upset or ill within the last few days? Such inquiries may help the parent to realize the leader's personal interest in each child.

This opportunity for brief chats with the parents should never be used for complaints about the child's misbehavior. If there is any discipline problem in the nursery class, usually it may be traced to one or two reasons. It may be misunderstanding on the part of the leader due to her own physical unfitness or to her lack of knowledge of the need and interest of little children. The second cause may be impending illness or physical strain, emotional stress, or exhaustion of the child.

When the inquiry is made in a tactful, sympathetic way, the parent understands that the leader is not complaining about the child, but has asked because of real interest. Frequently, the busy parent in the home does not realize just what is happening. Frances may not be feeling well, but she is not really ill. The nursery leader who notices that the child does not act in her usual happy way may help the parent to avert a serious illness.

On the other hand, the leader who meets the child only once a week needs the assistance and explanation that the parent offers so that the child may be more fully understood, his needs faced, and ways of meeting these needs more carefully considered.

The home is the first, the greatest, and the most lasting influence in the life of the child. The nursery leader wishes to supplement this work of the home. The leader needs to come close to the home life of the child. She needs to help the parents to know why she has planned an informal homelike situation in the church. Visits in the home and all friendly contacts with the parents or children help establish a confidence and understanding and a sense of comradeship in the common task of helping to guide the Christian nurture of young children.

6

Nursery Department Organization

THE CLASS FOR THREE-YEAR-OLDS IS A PART OF THE CHURCH
program for children under four. This text is prepared for the guidance of leaders of the class for three-year-olds and parents of these
children. It is well for these workers to know and understand the
service the church renders to children before they enter this class.
This service will vary according to community needs and attitudes,
number of families with young children in the church membership,
available space, and leadership.

Throughout the nursery years the nursery workers will serve the
child through service to his home. Beginning with its ministry to
youth, guidance in wise choice of mates, and in helping young people
to achieve Christian homes, the church attempts to help each child
to be well-born. It shares with the family in welcoming the child
and attempts to create a feeling that the child is a part of the church
fellowship. This work is carried out by nursery home visitors. The
leaflets,[1] *The Nursery Home Visitor at Work* (101-B) and *Dedicating
Young Children in Baptism* (100-C) should be read carefully by all
nursery workers.

One of the fine contributions the nursery home visitor can make
is to inform parents of services the church is prepared to render to
children under four and the organization through which it is done.
She will explain to the parents that children will not be promoted from
the nursery class until they are within two years of entering first grade
in public school. She may also prepare parents for the experiences
they may expect their children to have when they become old enough
to participate in group activities. Some parents, recalling church-
school experiences of their own childhood, probably at a period much
older than three, are not prepared to understand or appreciate the
informality of the church nursery class and mistake it for glorified
baby sitting.

Where space and facilities permit and where there is felt need for
such services, some churches provide care for infants and toddlers
during church school, worship services, and other adult activities.
Three-year-olds are included in such care during adult activities and
at times other than the regular Sunday morning class period. In many

---

[1] These may be secured from Service Department, Box 871, Nashville, Tennessee.

situations, a real need is met by such through-the-week care services. Unfortunately, in many churches, such nursery services are not carried on in a fashion conducive to happy development for the children. Often noise, disorder, even uncleanliness may be found. The workers who staff such nurseries are often untrained or called upon to serve more children of varied ages than is good.

The care services of the church are a part of the responsibility of the nursery department. Policies and practices concerning these should be carefully worked out in order to insure children maximum protection and happiness while being cared for.

An increasingly large number of churches now provide a class for two-year-olds. Parents and teachers should carefully study the material provided for this age group. There are differences of opinion as to whether or not the group for two-year-olds should be called a class or a care group. Whatever it is called, it should provide happy, wholesome experiences for two-year-olds.

Almost all churches now provide for a nursery class for the three-year-olds. While some of them enroll children not quite three, it is recommended that children be enrolled in this class about the time of the third birthday. Some children, of course, are not ready for group experiences that early, but most of them are. Where the church provides a group for two-year-olds, this will sometimes mean that children are promoted from group to group on the Sunday nearest the third birthday. Some churches may promote once a year. The children promoted to the three-year-old nursery class will be within three years of entering first grade of public school.

Where no group is provided for children younger than three, the nursery class workers will keep in touch with nursery home visitors, get acquainted with children in their homes and plan with parents for the child's entry into the nursery class at the time when he is ready. In churches with very few young children, the two groups are likely to be kept together. The workers will plan, in such situations, to furnish each family with the correct materials for use at home for each child according to his age. In the church-school group, through individual and small group activities, they will seek to provide each child with the guidance he needs.

Being part of a large group creates tensions for young children, so if there are as many as six or seven three-year-olds who attend church school, a separate room should be provided for them.

There should never be less than two workers during each session, even with a small group of three-year-olds. Some activities, such as looking at picture books, listening to stories, playing the piano and singing together, may keep a worker in one place. At least one worker should be free to move about, watching, listening, and entering into activities when children's needs indicate that she should do so. One worker for every four or five nursery class children is desirable. If the enrollment is twenty, for instance, at least four adults should work with the group. Five adults would be better and would provide greater opportunity for work with individuals.

When the average attendance in a group exceeds fifteen, it is well to consider organization of another nursery class, seeking through the commission on education additional space and leadership. Even though the nursery classroom is large and there are many workers, a crowd is likely to lead to overstimulation and to necessitate more formality in procedure. Occasionally, a group of teachers with a large group and a big space is able through careful planning, possibly division of space with bookshelves or piano, to provide small group activities which do not crowd each other, and to achieve a feeling of individual ease despite large attendance.

Church school sessions vary in length. Where three-year-olds remain at church during worship services in addition to the church-school time, at least one of the teachers should be on duty. Plans should be made to maintain the same orderly worthwhile procedures as established during the church-school time.

Occasional weekday play times at the church provide opportunities for teachers and children to know one another better and to share activities which may have been omitted on Sunday. Parents usually welcome the opportunity for their children to participate in such group activity. Only a few churches are sufficiently well staffed and equipped to provide worthwhile experiences for three-year-olds during vacation church-school sessions for older children. (See "Vacation Church School and the Three-year-old," page 89.)

Promotion

With the use of the Closely Graded Kindergarten Courses, an increasing number of churches provide two kindergarten groups, one for fours and one for fives. It is recommended that all children who will start to public school in two years shall enter the kindergarten for four-year-olds at the beginning of the church-school year. This means that some children are in the nursery class for less than a year, some for more than a year. Since the nursery class program is based upon individual and small group teaching, this is considered as better than promotion all through the year.

Promotion should be looked forward to as an evidence of growing older and becoming capable of doing things calling for greater skill and sustained attention. While those who are to be promoted are encouraged to look forward to this new experience with pleasure, care should be taken to remind those who will remain in the nursery class that they will soon be the biggest children in the room. Care should be taken to avoid having them feel inferior.

Name Tags

Name tags are a great help in identification of all of the children in the group. Some children in nursery class are irregular attendants. Often a substitute teacher may be helping in the group. It is well, therefore, to have name tags worn by all of the children.

Permanent tags may be purchased at school supply houses. These are blocks of plywood, two inches square with two holes on one side. Heavy yarn, enameled shoe strings, or ribbon may be slipped through the holes, to make a "tag necklace." The child's name may be printed on each tag. A gummed seal of a dog, bird, or some other attractive seal may be put on by the children.

Temporary name tags may be made of poster board and seals, but are only useful for a few sessions as they are easily torn.

Four-Year-Olds in the Group

Since most state laws or community regulations fix a date upon which a child's entry into public school is determined, and since his church-school work is closely related to that of his public-school grade, it is considered wise to keep children together in church school who are in the same grade of public school. The nursery class is considered to be the best group in which to make the division. Since this means that there will be a number of four-year-olds in the group for several months before promotion time, teaching procedures must be adapted to meet the needs of these older children while assimilating into the class those who are barely three. This may call for an increase in the number of the teachers, as well as careful planning for each session. Such plans might include a few games, additional music appreciation, singing and rhythm experiences, and books and stories of special interest to four-year-olds.

Teacher Responsibilities

Every person who works with nursery class children is a teacher. While one person may be leading teacher, all workers should study the session plans, share in planning, and feel themselves responsible for the individual welfare of children and the success of each session. Specific responsibilities may be assigned or assumed. One teacher may keep attendance records, make out reports, see that name tags are kept in order, and the offering prepared for the secretary of the church school. Another, a mothering person, man or woman, may be gifted in helping the unhappy, ill, or disturbed child to become adjusted. Another may be responsible for the piano, for sharing songs and conversation with children who are interested. Others may be responsible, or turns may be taken, in caring for equipment, having the room ready before the children come, seeing that toys are clean, safe, and ready for use. While all teachers should be free to move about as children's interests demand, in some situations it has been found good to have teachers assume responsibility for certain areas of interest, such as housekeeping, block play, books, puzzles, big muscle equipment, or outdoor activities.

Designation of responsibilities should be part of the outcome of planning sessions together. As teachers meet in their room to work together, cleaning, mending, straightening equipment and supplies, planning for sessions, and ways of rendering better services to children, they will find themselves growing spiritually and in enthusiasm for their task. Part of each workers' meeting should be devoted to discussing individual children and their needs. Care should be taken to avoid criticism of parents. Skilled leading teachers will find such sessions provide opportunities to guide less skillful workers to read materials which will enrich their lives spiritually, broaden their understanding of children, unfold better ways of teaching, and provide help in dealing with specific problems.

In addition to meetings with their own group, nursery class teachers will participate in general workers' meetings and leadership classes. No group functions apart from the remainder of the church program. Nursery class teachers need to see the whole church program clearly in order to understand their own share in it.

7

Room and Equipment

THE WORD "FUNCTIONAL" IS POPULAR TODAY AMONG THOSE WHO plan houses, buildings for factories, offices, and schools. In planning a room for three-year-olds, workers should think in terms of what is supposed to take place in that room in order that children's needs may be met to the fullest advantage. It should be a room that allows for a maximum of child activity with the least danger to child health and safety, and which minimizes the necessity for rules and restrictions. It should be attractive, conveniently located, and should have in it such furniture and equipment as will contribute to the growth and development of children.

The nursery classroom should be located on the ground floor if possible. If it is necessary that it be on a higher floor, the stairs should be easy to climb, with railing placed at proper height for three-year-old children. If the room must be a basement room, stairs should be easy to climb and well lighted. The floors and walls must be dry. Lighting experts can place lights so that there will be no feeling of being shut in or of being underground. Teachers should know where parents are so that they may be found quickly and easily if they are needed. Hallways should be well lighted. Easy access to outdoor space is desirable.

Toilet facilities should be easily accessible. It is desirable to have toilet rooms adjoining the nursery classroom. Fixtures should be small and low enough for children to be comfortable and independent in their use. If small toilets and wash basins are not available, boxes or stools should be provided upon which children may stand. The paper towel and toilet paper dispensers should be within easy reach. Workers should know the vocabulary by which a child evidences his need for going to the toilet. Such help as is needed should be given in matter-of-fact fashion, while children are encouraged to learn to help themselves.

Since activity is almost constant at three, the nursery classroom should be large enough to allow freedom to move about. Thirty-five square feet of floor space per child is recommended. For better separation of noise-producing and quiet activities, a rectangular room is generally considered better than a square one. In order to maintain space for movement, workers are wise to avoid filling floor space with too much furniture. Tables with small chairs are desirable for books, puzzles, or clay. If floor space is limited, one table may be used. Large blocks or boxes may also serve for these purposes. A washable rug or quilt may be used for sitting on the floor. It can be put away when floor space is needed for other activities. Heavy linoleum floor covering is easy to keep clean, sound absorbing and attractive. Where the floor is well heated, such floor covering increases possibilities for floor play.

Provision should be made for storage of hats, purses, rain boots, and other possessions. This may be inside the room if space permits. A shelf with a rod and coat hangers will provide for hanging wraps and placing of hats, gloves, and purses. Teachers will need to help the child put his coat on a hanger, but by doing so she will be providing training in the correct way of hanging a coat.

A picture rail or picture board should be provided. Several short strips are preferable so that pictures may be used in various parts of the room. If cork board is used, it may be hung so that the bottom extends several inches from the wall, thus providing a sloping surface which may be used as an easel for drawing or painting. The rack at the bottom should be wide for displaying mounted pictures.

Windows should be of clear glass and low enough to permit children to see out, or steps may be placed under those which are high. Window ledges should be wide enough to be used for placing pictures, interesting nature material, and growing plants. If windows may be opened from the top for ventilation, with the lower panes fastened securely, children are not tempted to go in and out through them. Dutch (half) doors into corridors or hallways are desirable, permitting those who wish to see in, while the bottom part remains closed to prevent children leaving the room unobserved. A pane of clear glass in the upper half of the door helps when the entire door is kept closed for comfort or to prevent the noise likely to be made in the nursery class from disturbing other groups.

The nursery classroom should be well ventilated and kept as comfortable as possible. Since three-year-olds live at floor level, it is well to have a thermometer placed on a baseboard. The temperature there should be about seventy degrees. Children are likely to be warm-natured and active, and adult feelings are not always the best guide to room temperature control.

Floor coverings should be easy to keep clean and sanitary, should be comfortable for children to sit on, and should be attractive in appearance. Some churches have found hardwood or carpeting usable, but in general some of the rubber tile or linoleum coverings are considered more desirable. Some of these may be laid satisfactorily on concrete basement floors. It would be wise for a church group to consult a building contractor or engineer before spending large sums on floor coverings. Advances and improvements are being made in this area and the church should take advantage of these.

A washable rug which may be spread for looking at books, or in a play area may help to make floor play more desirable. These floor coverings should be washed frequently and rolled up when not in use. Teachers should dress comfortably in clothes in which they, too, may sit on the floor with ease.

Storage space for supplies and a place where teachers may put away their wraps should be easily accessible. While toys are kept constantly available, certain materials and some toys are likely to be kept out of reach of the children and brought out when they are to be used. This prevents their unwise use and abuse. Many materials which have value to three-year-olds when used occasionally under adult guidance, can become a source of annoyance or real danger if used indiscriminately.

Open shelves so built that they will not tip over, should be provided to make blocks and small toys available for children at all times. These may be placed under windows, along the wall, or may extend into the room to form partitions between centers of activity.

Boxes for toys or blocks encourage disorder and are not as good as shelves. If the room is used for other purposes during the week, shelves may be turned to the wall, or hinged together in sections which may be kept closed.

All equipment should be safe and sturdy. Flimsy items do not last long enough in the nursery class to justify their purchase. A piece of equipment to be used in the nursery class must be strong enough to support the weight of a man.

Centers likely to be included in most nursery classrooms are: housekeeping play, play with blocks and small toys, play with large blocks, big muscle play, books, pictures, puzzles. Puzzles for the younger children should have not more than five or six pieces. By the end of the year many nursery class children can work with ease a puzzle with twelve to fifteen pieces. Use of creative art materials will be occasional rather than regular, and an area for their use may be set up upon occasion. This may be a low table, at an easel, on the floor, or on the top of a toy shelf.

In the housekeeping area, there may be a small tea table, though

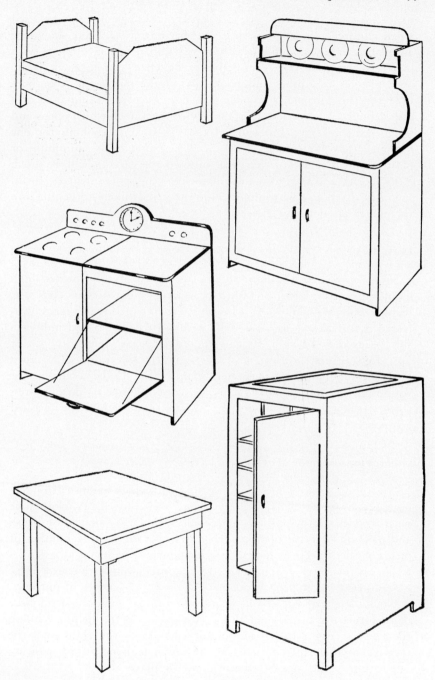

many workers prefer to have a larger table which may be used when children play at preparing and sharing meals. There should be a doll bed, large enough for a three-year-old to get in himself, with mattress and coverings. A small rocking chair is welcomed. If no open shelves for dishes and books are in the portion of the room used for this purpose, a wooden box may be painted and used as a dish cabinet. A stove (see page 55), with oven door which opens and shuts and some pots and pans of the size used in cooking for one person, a few tablespoons, a set of dishes, preferably aluminum or plastic, and a small pitcher and unbreakable glasses will be used. A tablecloth and napkins add to homelike atmosphere. Knives, forks, spoons, baby bottle with nipples, and other toys likely to be put into the mouth are not wise choices.

Dolls

Several inexpensive dolls about twelve to sixteen inches high including a baby doll are quite satisfactory for nursery class use. Rubber dolls with movable arms and legs and painted eyes are preferred. Unbreakable dolls, or dolls with stuffed bodies and unbreakable heads may be used. Clothes should be large enough to permit easy dressing and undressing. Large snaps are the most satisfactory fastenings. Squares of cloth and blanket should be available for wrapping the dolls as young children often cannot or do not dress them. Doll clothing should be simple and should be washed frequently.

Other Housekeeping Toys

An ironing board which does not fold and which has a shelf underneath, and several small, simple irons are enjoyed. A clothesline with wooden clothespins may be used at times. A small dust brush and pan should be available. Rather than having a large number of pieces of furniture which serve only one purpose, it is considered good to have a few pieces, supplemented by painted wooden boxes or large blocks (16x22x4 inches) which may be used for a variety of purposes. A block may be a bed, a table, or a dressing table, while the small piece of furniture can be only one thing. Not only does this help in making the best use of limited space, but it encourages the children to be creative in their use of materials. A toy telephone affords visiting opportunities and may be used in dramatic play.

Tables and Chairs

While nursery children enjoy working and playing on the floor, they also like small tables and chairs. Rectangular tables with hard tops, eighteen inches high may be purchased. Avoid tables with a wide apron under top surface. Correct posture chairs (8 inches high) are recommended. About eight chairs should be enough for use with a group whose attendance does not exceed fifteen as it is not necessary to provide for every child to be seated at the same time. Large blocks may be used to sit on, too.

Pictures

One or two framed pictures may be hung at eye level of the children. These are best framed simply and without glass. Reflection sometimes prevents children from seeing a glass-covered picture clearly. There is also the danger from broken glass. A picture of Jesus as a baby with his mother may hang in the housekeeping area; another of Jesus and the children may hang elsewhere. Young children prefer that the baby have on clothing and that the full picture of the mother be seen. Some teachers have found it wise to select a picture from the nursery class picture set. The more simple the picture and the fewer the details, the better.

In the picture set, *Nursery Class Pictures,* accompanying this course, there will not be a picture for each session. The pupils' books and the smaller pictures on *My Picture Card* (the weekly take-home piece) will supplement the large pictures. The pictures may be clipped from the pupils' books, mounted, and hung at the eye level of the child or placed on a table. Teachers will also use pictures clipped from magazines.

Books

A few well-chosen books dealing with Jesus the Baby and the Friend, with home life, and with nature, may be used year in and year out. A few others which will contribute directly to the emphasis of the season may be added and removed from time to time. It is an error to have a large number of books for young children to mishandle and which do not contribute to the accomplishment of the purposes of the nursery class. Durable homemade picture books, with pictures built around one interest, as pets, family, and so on, are valuable. Lists of books for children will be found in current issues of *Child Guidance in Christian Living*.

Puzzles

A few simple puzzles may be enjoyed, especially by the older children in the group. Puzzle type educational toys, such as the mailbox into which blocks of various shapes are placed in slots of corresponding shape; color cones, nests of boxes, and other small individual toys are good especially for the youngest children in the group. A basket, a plastic pail, a box in which to keep small toys is worthwhile.

Piano

While neither a piano nor a record player is considered necessary in the nursery class, either or both can contribute much. Their use will be discussed elsewhere. (See pages 71 and 76.)

Big Muscle Equipment

Even with limited, crowded space some pieces of big muscle equipment should be provided. In addition to big, strong trucks, and other moving toys, there should be something upon which young children may climb. However, if space is very limited it is an error to permit one piece of equipment to dominate that space throughout the year. Perhaps a small indoor slide may be used for a few Sundays, then stored, in order to prevent sliding from becoming the only activity of the class. A low wooden bench or short walking board is the simplest form of big muscle equipment and may be used to climb on and jump from, to outline a play house, as a train, a bus, or a pew for playing church. A rocking boat or an indoor gym provides opportunity for children to play in groups and begin to learn to share.

Large trucks, floor trains, and boats will encourage imaginative play involving use of big muscles.

In some situations where indoor space is limited, big muscle equipment is kept stored during the week and placed in a fellowship hall, gymnasium, or in some other space used for other purposes during the week. All or some of the three-year-olds may be taken there for a little while to enjoy using these on Sunday morning.

AN EVALUATION OF SOME NURSERY CLASS TOYS

RELIGIOUS VALUES	SOCIAL VALUES	PHYSICAL VALUES

DOLLS—WITH REMOVABLE CLOTHES AND BLANKETS
(INCLUDING TOY CATS, DOGS, AND TEDDY BEARS)

Mother care, pure joy, frequent opportunities for songs, occasional opportunities for prayer, setting up home patterns.	Sharing, taking turns, beginning to play together in small groups, bringing doll from home and letting others play with it.	Handling carefully, dressing and undressing, carrying around.

BLOCKS · BLOCKS · BLOCKS

Basis for innumerable good times together as garages, roads, churches, towers, houses, chairs, and so on, are built. Frequent conversation-center. Many opportunities afforded for waiting for use of certain blocks, learning not to hold too long, nor retain too many, learning to return blocks to shelf after use. Weekly center of interest adds stimuli for creative expression.

BOOKS · BOOKS · BOOKS

Pictures may lead to stories —as Christmas story, or Jesus and the children. Associated with home activities, play and other children may help develop sense of security.	Enjoying together, sharing, taking turns, conversation center, opportunity to show favorite book brought from home.	Manipulation—learning to handle with care.

BALLS · BALLS · BALLS

Help in developing sense of security as this favorite home toy is associated with church school. First discovery of church as a friendly place may be through ball play.	Rolling to one another as a means of learning names. Enjoying together. Means whereby older children may show friendliness to younger.	Manipulation—muscular control of arm muscles. Coordination of arms and legs. Controlled manipulation, ball is rolled or bounced indoors, thrown when outdoors.

HOUSEKEEPING TOYS · HOUSEKEEPING TOYS · HOUSEKEEPING TOYS

Follow home patterns. Provide opportunities for conversation, stories, songs, prayers.	Playing in small groups. Taking share of certain responsibilities. Discussion as to ways of housekeeping.	Motor control. Learning to use some toys in right ways, as dishes, blankets, broom, sweeper, and so on.

SMALL TOYS · SMALL TOYS · SMALL TOYS
(THESE INCLUDE TRUCKS, AUTOS, FLOOR TRAIN, AND OTHER EDUCATIONAL TOYS.)

May be basis for discovering friendly world beyond home. Give confidence to child— sense of security—here are toys similar to his toys at home.	Conversation center, opportunity for discovering friends in church school. Need for sharing.	Manipulation—and definitely planning use for toys.

SLIDE, ROCKING BOAT, STEPS

Under skilled leadership religious values are evident—then these may be centers for conversation, songs, and prayers.

Opportunities for taking turns, waiting for one another. Conversation center.

Exercise for larger muscles.

Outdoor Play Space

More and more churches are recognizing the value of providing outdoor play space for use by young children. Such space should be made safe through fencing, have some shade, and be located in such a place as to permit children to play freely without disturbing those in classes indoors. Such a play space does not need to be very large to provide a great deal of pleasure and many opportunities for children to learn better ways of getting along with others his own age in real life situations. Equipment should be as safe as possible and should be usable by children in quick succession or at the same time. It should permit much play without the need for many restrictions or rules, though adults will be constantly alert to see that children are safe and to take advantage of learning situations.

There may be an additional small area of the playground reserved for digging and planting bulbs and seeds. If there is no playground, such a planting area may be located elsewhere on the church property. Even a very small space, approximately 36x18 inches, may provide opportunities for rich experiences in religious growth as three-year-olds begin to sense the wonder of blooming bulbs and sprouting seeds and thus to recognize God as creator.

Some suggested outdoor playground equipment includes: climbing apparatus, several rope swings with canvas or leather seats, a slide, big outdoor building blocks, a few planks, low sawhorses, a teeter-totter with circular base to prevent bumps. All equipment should be kept in good repair and well painted.

Such a list of suggested equipment may be overwhelming in prospect for the church with very limited space and little money to spend. As in our family and personal situations, it is good to know what is ideal, what we have to work with and to make choices as we gradually work toward achieving the ideal. Much equipment can be built by the do-it-yourself craftsman at less cost than that purchased from educational furniture and supply manufacturers. It is better to get a little at a time and be sure that what is bought or made is strong, sturdy, safe, and long lasting than to provide a lot of flimsy equipment at once and have it prove unsatisfactory.

Careful planning for each session will help even the overcrowded situation. Some churches have divided their groups and use the same space at different hours for each of them. Others alternate in use of indoor and outdoor space during one session in order to avoid overstimulation and overcrowding.

As the program for children is strengthened, and as adults recognize the devotion and skill of those who are working with and for their children, more money and more space may become available.

8

Some Teaching Techniques

LIVING TOGETHER IN A HAPPY SITUATION PROVIDES YOUNG CHILDREN with many learning opportunities. There are ways, however, in which teachers may through guidance insure children of opportunities to grow and develop happily through association with the group. First of all, teachers must recognize that good sessions and lessons to be put over are not the objective of the nursery class. Very seldom will the whole group come together to listen to instructions or receive information from a teacher. Rather, each child will be treated as an individual, allowed to develop according to his own readiness and tempo, and encouraged to find his own way independently. A friendly sympathetic adult can help each child do this. Teachers should be alert and available at all times. During the session there is no time for adult visiting.

When children come into the classroom they should be greeted in a friendly way, encouraged to help with removing and putting away wraps, caps, and purses, and invited to find something pleasant to do. This may include walking about, looking at things with the teacher, handling objects, listening and being listened to. Even a very small child often has something to say as soon as he arrives.

The teacher who will sit or stoop down to his level, pay careful attention, and make appropriate comments, is likely to win his confidence. Some children need little urging to make themselves at home with other children and avail themselves of the toys. Others have been taught not to touch anything until they are told and so need to be reminded often: "You may play with the things in this room. They are for all the boys and girls." If and when a child finds a toy or an activity in which he is interested, he should be permitted to stop and enjoy it. An alert teacher will be able to see when he is in need of a change and may suggest that he move on to another activity. Sometimes the sentence-type story or song about a picture, or something seen through the window provides the best opportunity of the session for this kind of teacher sharing. Or, it may prove to be helpful in suggesting to the child some activity from which he may gain pleasure. For instance, a teacher pauses before a picture of Jesus as a baby, hanging over the doll bed, and tells the child how Jesus' family loved him and looked after him when he was a baby. She

Photograph by Patty Chadwell

compares it with the love and care he has received when he was a
baby, and says, "You play taking care of the doll babies like that."
Perhaps the idea appeals to him, and he will wish to stay in the housekeeping area, putting the dolls to bed, or sitting in the rocking chair,
listening while the teacher sings to him about Jesus as a baby.

Sometimes, several children and a teacher will walk about the
room together, pausing to look out of the window and talk about
the birds. Some food may be provided which they will place on the

bird feeder outside the window. Or, they may tell of birds which eat outside the windows at their own homes. They may examine an abandoned nest and hear that it is part of God's plan that each creature knows how to build itself a home.

Through the give and take of this kind of informal moving about, looking, handling, talking, and listening, much of the best teaching in the nursery class is done. This is not constant for soon young children become occupied in their own pursuits and are best left alone by teachers. For such occupation, floor toys—interlocking trains without wheels, boats, a wagon made of a box with casters, small blocks, large blocks for building, trucks, and put-together toys—are made available.

Group play may be suggested or encouraged, but is not insisted upon. Young children enjoy play near one another without actually playing together. They are imitative, however. When one child has placed large blocks in a line and begins to march about on them, others are likely to join in.

Picture books should be placed at several places in the room. A book about family life or one about Jesus as a baby should be available for use in the doll corner. A book of nature pictures may be placed on the shelf or table with nature items, such as shells and nests. A book about builders or road workers may be near the blocks. Others may be placed on a table or rug where children may examine them alone, or with a teacher to talk about them or read from them. Simple puzzles may be available. A song book may be enjoyed at the piano or away from it. One child or several may listen or join in as a teacher sings.

Worship

While some Bible stories and some songs mentioning God and Jesus will be used often, there will be no conscious effort to teach Bible content. The child who attends the nursery class regularly should become familiar with the words God and Jesus. These words should be related to happy experiences which the child learns to think of as part of God's plans for his world. He may come to know that the Bible is a special book that tells us about God, and which has in it the stories about Jesus. Some nursery class teachers like to have an attractive copy of the Bible within sight and reach of teachers and children during every session. Some of them choose brightly-covered copies, red or blue. Others prefer white or black leather. While the

Bible may be kept on a low table near the offering basket, with a bowl of flowers, this is not a worship center. Symbols such as candles and crosses are not understood by such young children and should not be used with them.

Teachers will watch for any opportunity which may present itself to share with children moments of wonder and joy, during which there may be feelings which are worshipful. This may come as dolls are put to bed, as a child plays doctor or nurse or mother, and a teacher says, "I'm glad God plans for so many people to help take care of babies." She may wish to use such a time for a prayer sentence. Or, it may come when bulbs which have been kept in a dark place all week are taken out and the exciting discovery is made that they are "waking up" by putting out new shoots which are ready now for exposure to light.

Sometimes a small group of children may move quickly from active play to a quiet time of listening and thinking out of which a worship experience may grow. One teacher says that she often plays a game with three or four of her children in which she sings to them, telling them various things to do as they hold hands in a circle. They may move around on tiptoe, or jump up and down, or move very slowly. After a time she sings the suggestion that they sit on the floor and shut their eyes. When they are quiet and relaxed she makes a comment about how good it is to have a church where we have such happy times together. She sings a song of thanks for friends at church who sing and play. Or she may tell a story, have a prayer, or just suggest that we rest and think about our nice church. Since play is the business of childhood, making worship a natural companion of it is good teaching.

One wise mother has said, "I want my child's religion to enter his life and change it's flavor, just as the vanilla changes the flavor of the cake batter. I don't want it smoothed over the outside like the icing."

Using Big Muscle Equipment

Learning through the use of big muscle equipment has already been discussed, but it should be kept in mind that development of physical skill and pride in one's achievement are an important part of child development. Learning good ways of using equipment and respecting the rights of others as children share in its use are valuable. Teachers do well to work out a few suggestions for using the equipment, repeating the same phrases over and over rather than using many new words with three-year-olds. For instance, one group sings, "Taking turns in work and play makes us happy every day." In another group, in the same situation, the teacher may repeat over and over again, "*Up* the steps and *down* the slide! Each one takes a turn." One set of words is not superior to the other, but it is good to choose one and stay with it until the desired response is learned.

In such situations the young child begins to learn that he is important and has rights but that others also have rights, and so he must take turns. Too often he is urged to share before he feels secure in his own rights. It is unwise to demand mature behavior from immature persons. If an adult takes something from a nursery child, hands it to another child, saying, "You must share," the child has not actually shared it. He has been overpowered by superior strength. Often he resents both the adult behavior and the child who is the recipient of the "generosity." The opposite of good will is set up.

On the other hand, when "togetherness" has really been enjoyed it may be verbalized in some such manner as this, "Haven't we had fun?" "It is good to have a church school where we can play with our friends and share our toys and take turns on the slide." The song,

"Thank you, God, this happy day,
For friends at church who sing and play,"

may be used in an almost unlimited number of situations.

Excursions

Occasional excursions outside their room may prove pleasant and profitable for three-year-olds. A walk around the outside of the church building, stopping to look at and hear about the steeple, bell tower, or air conditioning units, with a pause for talking and resting, provides opportunity for understanding the bigness of the church. A visit to the sanctuary to sit in adult pews and look at the windows is most worthwhile.

No child should be urged to join an excursion. If he prefers to remain in the room, let him do so. At least one adult worker should remain in the room with children who do not care to join a proposed excursion.

If the group goes outside the building where they may be close to busy streets, there should be at least one adult for every three or four children. Before leaving the room, children should understand why they are asked to walk quietly and stay together. While some workers object to it as depriving a child of his individual enjoyment of a walk, others have found the safety of a so-called "rope walk," worthwhile. Rope or tape is provided, with each child holding it as he walks along. Four or five children may hold the tape, two on one side holding the tape with their right hands, two or three on the other side, holding the tape with their left hands. A teacher should hold one end or the middle of each tape. There will thus be opportunity for the small group to have conversation with the teacher. Loops tied in the tape at intervals of two feet help regulate the distance between the children.

In some situations it has been found practicable to have one or two adults take a few of the children at a time for an excursion rather than to have the whole class go at one time. For example, in a downtown church, situated at the intersection of two busy streets, teachers wished children to have a little visit outside to feel the push and sting of the March wind, and to look for evidences of spring's approach. Two teachers took small groups outside, warmly buttoned up with coats and caps. As they stood against the side of the church building they saw signs moving in the wind and adults hurrying along holding their hats. The children found some tiny green plants and white flowers pushing up between cracks of the church walk. Just inside the door of the church they stopped again to look out at bits of paper blowing along the street and noted the flutter of a window curtain. To have taken the entire group would have provided little pleasure to any of them. With a few at a time it was pleasant and worthwhile.

In another situation, two or three children were taken to the back of the church where a bird had built a nest in a bush. One at a time they stood on a box to peep at the nest. Back on the steps they talked of it and listened to a story about Jesus and the birds. When they went back to the room, another small group went out to see the wonderful nest.

Visitors

Some community helpers, such as the postman, a police officer, a doctor, or a nurse, may make an interesting contribution by visiting in the nursery class. The minister, caretaker of the building, and other members of the church staff should become known through frequent short visits. While such visits will be treated more fully in the

Sunday-by-Sunday session plans which follow, there are some general ideas concerning visitors which teachers would do well to consider.

First, the object of such a visit is to help children know, appreciate, and enjoy these adult friends. In order that this may be achieved, workers should plan with the adult visitor, letting him know what is expected of him. If children can continue with their usual activities with the visitor moving about from one small group to another, being introduced and having an opportunity to speak to the children as individuals, he is more likely to relax and be informal and natural in his approach to them. One friendly police officer sat down on a walking board and listened for some time as a group of children told him about how carefully they crossed the streets. After listening he told them he was glad that they were careful and glad that he could help them to know how and when to cross at a busy corner, with their mothers. After a friendly doctor had visited, one group of three-year-olds played hospital in the housekeeping area. They seemed quite happy when their teacher said a prayer of thanks for good doctors who work to help us keep well.

Clean-up Activities

Cleaning up after work should become an accepted part of procedure. It is not wise to make children clean up as punishment. Nor is it necessary that a child shall always clean up what he himself has mussed up and never that which was left by someone else. The teacher will give encouragement and will help with straightening. The important thing is to be sure that every child enters into activities, including that of cleaning up "our" room in order to keep it a nice-looking place.

Oftentimes, if a child is forced to come back and put away toys before moving on to the next activity, his interest in the new challenge is lost while he cleans up after the old one. Cleaning in order that we may have room for something that we wish to do or in order that we may leave our room looking neat is desirable.

Be careful to provide something interesting to do after cleaning up at the close of a session. Children who have been securely happy may become upset if their parents do not come for them immediately when teachers indicate that the session is over. It is better for teachers to finish straightening the room after the children have gone than to spoil a session for a child by having him become dissatisfied while he waits with nothing to do at the end of the session. Since not all parents come at the same time, teachers will watch carefully to see that each child is busy and happy until it is time for him to go. Any formal closing for the session is out of place. Regardless of time schedules or bells, the session begins for each child when he comes and ends when he leaves, and teachers will watch that both the beginning and close of the child's experience are satisfying.

Teachers will learn through trial and error, ways of helping children find satisfactory occupation in the nursery class. They may read books recommended in *Child Guidance in Christian Living* to find ways of developing techniques in guidance of children. Principally, the young child needs to be aware of the nearness and availability of the help of the sympathetic adult who will listen, suggest, and leave him alone at times. Teachers should have ready a number of usable brief stories, or be ready to make one up. They should know the stories and songs in the lesson material and use them when they seem suitable. They should be ready to make up and sing words which suggest suitable activity or emotional reaction to situations. They should have on hand pictures, books, and other materials with which to enrich children's experiences. But they should be careful not to be dominating or teaching all the time.

Sometimes the teacher may suggest or initiate an activity, leaving it to the children if they are interested. Children often become bored with or tired of an activity without realizing it, and the alert, watchful teacher may suggest a change. The group that becomes too noisy may be guided to quieter activity, or the child or children who engage for a long time in an activity which has become dull may be encouraged to try out some more interesting pursuit. For example: John had put blocks into and out of the mail box for a long time. Occasionally he would look at other children, then go back to his own occupation. A teacher put a few pieces of paper into a bag and suggested to John that he might like to be the postman and deliver these letters to the people in the housekeeping area.

A group of children in the rocking boat began to bump, to tumble in and out and squeal noisily. A teacher suggested that the captain should be sure to stop his boat each time a passenger got in or out. She suggested a place for the boat to go and sang a little quiet song about having a good time in the boat. A more orderly spirit took over the group.

Mary carefully placed large blocks to form a circle. The teacher took her hand and walked around the circle, singing about a merry-go-round which went round and round. Two or threee children fell in step and played the game. After a while the teacher suggested that they all sit down for a rest. She told them a story about children who had fun playing together in nursery class. She said a prayer of gladness for fun in church school. Mary's placing of the blocks had perhaps been purely physical and mechanical. The teacher utilized what she had built to give Mary more pleasure and to include other children. The opportunity for the rest time, story, and prayer followed naturally.

Sometimes seasonal changes will provide teachers with opportunities for helping children learn and grow. When nights become cool in the early fall, new blankets will be welcomed in the housekeeping area and provide opportunities for teachers to suggest gladness for comfortable homes. Changes in plant life, flowers, and wearing apparel will be of interest with each change of season. If we who have watched spring, summer, fall, and winter come and go for a number of years, still find in this evidence of the dependability of God's world and rejoice in it, we will appreciate it still more as it is shared with young children to whom it is a new experience.

Sometimes opportunities for learning and enjoying new experiences will be arranged by teachers. This may be introduced by adding new and interesting equipment or play material, inviting a guest, or providing some creative art material that is not usually available. When this is done, teachers should plan together as to how these new experiences may be made valuable to the children.

Some teachers feel that the environment should provide the stimulus for children's activities almost exclusively and that teachers should remain almost entirely in the background. Others feel that teachers should be alert for every opportunity to enter into children's experiences to enrich, interpret, and guide. No one can make rules which are absolutely right for all groups, all the time. Each teacher and each group of teachers will by study, planning, working together, and evaluating, arrive at their own best performance. Mistakes will be made, for human judgment is often erroneous, but wise workers will learn from their mistakes. Experience will bring an increase in skill if workers continue to study, are willing to change, and constantly keep in mind the best interests of the children.

9

Music in the Nursery Class

SINGING IS ONE OF THE NATURAL EXPERIENCES FOR YOUNG CHILDREN to enjoy. Humming, or singing little made-up, repetitious songs as they play will occur frequently among happy children. A teacher who sings finds it easy to join in these songs. A noted British psychologist has said that the mother who sings to her child is not likely to yell at him. Music, like other activities, should be used throughout the sessions by all workers, not reserved for a special time when all the children come together. It is not recommended that all of the children will ever be brought together for musical experiences.

Use of a Piano

A piano may be very helpful in the nursery class, but it is not a necessary piece of equipment. If a piano is provided, it should be well-tuned and kept in good condition. It should be used wisely under teacher guidance, not left open for children to bang upon. The children may be taught to press the keys with one or two fingers.

A good musician can enrich the experience of the group by playing for rest times, for rhythmic play, and for singing games. Children like to sit beside her on the piano bench, to examine the pictures which tell them what the songs are about, or to allow the teacher to guide their hands over the keyboard as she sings the words to them.

Singing Games

Organized games have no place with nursery children. But a teacher may catch hold of the hands of a single child or several may hold hands and begin to play "Ring Rosy" or "Getting Ready for Nursery Class," as an introduction to small group activity. Games *begin* in the nursery class, they are not organized or explained in advance. If the musician, seeing the activity, will begin to play, it will become a better game. Other children seeing the fun, may wish to join in. If so, other teachers may join them, too, but children should not be urged to leave other activities in which they are interested.

Sometimes a game is started to provide interest for one child. One little girl stood with her fingers in her mouth. A teacher caught both her hands and began to sing,

"Here we go up and here we go down
Teeter, totter to _____ town."

She named the town where the child's grandmother lived and to which the child paid frequent visits. Soon both teacher and child were playing the game with extended arms as they faced one another. Turning to bring another child into the play, the teacher asked, "Where does your grandmother live?" Then she sang about that town. No mention was made that fingers do not belong in mouths. The insecurity or boredom which had caused the finger sucking was relieved by enjoyment of the game. This teacher, recognizing boredom or insecurity, set about to remedy the cause for the undesirable behavior, instead of scolding.

Young children may not do more than one thing at a time. If they are moving about to music in a singing game or rhythmical play, they do not always sing. This means that the teacher must sing for them as she shares the activity. She may become exhausted long before the children are ready for a change of pace or activity. If an observant pianist provides the musical background and sings the words while another teacher joins in the activity, it will be more pleasant for all.

At three, children play for fun. Competition should not enter their games. Teachers will try to make as few rules as possible. A child who tires of playing, may leave the game at will.

Quiet Music

After a few moments of active play, the teacher may sit down on the floor, saying that she would like now to listen to some quiet music. This may be provided by a pianist or a record player may be used. If there are words the teacher and children will sing. Or, they may simply enjoy listening while they rest. Such a time of quiet relaxation for this small group may lead naturally to a story or prayer. Other groups in various parts of the room may have similar experiences. From this, children may go back to various individual interests in play centers. Here teachers may take advantage of opportunities to sing songs about friends, or about the play that is taking place.

Quiet music and rest times are needed during nearly every session. Most workers do not feel, however, that regular rest times for all children are needed during one-hour sessions. For longer sessions, and in through-the-week nursery schools, it is good to have a time of quiet resting, and if desired, music can be used. If the session is an extended one a rest time should be provided.

Children respond more readily if asked to share something than if told to do something. If the leading teacher will sit or lie down on the floor, using a towel or mat for a head rest, suggesting that she needs to rest and inviting children to join her, some of them will do so. It is best that all mats be identical to prevent unhappy confusion as children search for their own. These should be washable and kept clean. Each child should be given a paper napkin or paper towel to place on the mat under his head. The leading teacher should remain on the floor, talking or singing to children as they join her. Helpers should move quietly around the room, speaking softly to other children, telling them that it is time to rest and suggesting that they join the group. As soon as possible the helping teachers will rest, also. If blinds or curtains are drawn, shutting out light, rest is more acceptable. If children lie or sit quietly, it is not necessary that all of them stretch out, nor should they be urged to close their eyes.

The piano or record player may provide soothing background music. However, the voice of the teacher is likely to have as good an effect as any other means of gaining relaxation if she speaks soothingly and monotonously.

One teacher might stretch out on the floor and say, "I like to stretch on the floor. I like to close my eyes and be very, very quiet. I can feel myself resting." Since a long period of complete silence can be disturbing to young children, she might in a few moments begin to tell them a story or sing to a soft accompaniment some familiar songs and lullabies. After a while, she might suggest, "Let us sit up and listen together. I will tell you a story." Or she may sing up and down the scale, "Time to get up, time to get up." A drink of cool water may be served each child before he returns to activities. Some good records for such listening times are, Tschaikovsky's "Swan Ballet," MacDowell's "To a Water Lily" and "To a Wild Rose," and Brahm's "Lullaby."

When a Child Sings

Accompaniments are likely to confuse rather than help the young child learn to sing. Teachers sing to nursery children, but should not urge them to join in. They will do so when they are ready. Some will sing the songs they have heard when they go home, most of them will make up their own songs and sing them as they move around the nursery classroom or play at home.

Listen to a young child as he plays alone. Perhaps he sings about riding a pony as he dashes about on a broomstick horse, or hums unintelligible words as he plays with a toy on the floor.

Every teacher should know several simple songs to sing often to the children. She will use those in the pupils' books and others suited to the experiences of nursery class children.

Teachers sometimes complain that songs written for young children are pitched too high for the teachers to sing them naturally. For a long time it was commonly believed that the singing voices of young children were high. Interesting studies made at the Child Development Institute, Teachers College, Columbia University, and at Iowa Child Welfare Station, State University of Iowa, disagree with this belief.

If you will listen to children, you will realize that they often sing in a conversational tone, speaking the words on the note, in fact. Writers of songs for young children today are more likely to use the range from middle C to D than to pitch the songs higher.

Long ago adults felt that to learn to sing the great hymns of the church, no matter what experiences they interpreted, was good for young children. They said that children were thus storing up valuable worship material for use in later life. Then came a time when many songs were written about children and taught to them. They dealt with many symbols, comparing children to sunbeams, lambs, and flowers. Adults may think of children in such terms when they are being sentimental, but children do not think of themselves in this fashion. Such symbolism has been abandoned today by thoughtful students of early childhood.

Following this period of song making, writers of music for children were very careful that melodies were of good quality, that the experiences and ideas were suited to the age level of the child who was to learn the song, and that the vocabulary was within his range. Many lovely songs were written for and enjoyed by children. Some of them continue to be popular with both children and teachers.

Today the trend is to listen to children, to make up or learn simple songs to sing to and with them, and to encourage them to sing to us. The alert, creative teacher may pick up words or phrases from conversation or by listening to the child sing to himself, and by shortening a sentence, reshaping a phrase, or adding a word to make a rhyme, may produce singable songs which are essentially the children's creation. The *Singing Time* books by Coleman and Thorn contain many examples of such songs.

For the inexperienced teacher making her own songs may seem overwhelmingly difficult, even impossible. If that is the case, she will continue to use those written by others. But if she will try, she may discover that "making music" is an enriching experience for her and for the children she teaches.

A day school teacher observed a child having fun patting clay into a flat saucer-like shape then pressing his hand into it. She picked up his hand, laid it in her own and told him that no two people have hands just exactly alike. She mentioned some of the things he could do with his hands, ending the conversation with, "Aren't you glad for your hands?" Very seriously, he replied, "I'm very glad about all of me." The teacher then sang,

> "Hands to work with, eyes to see
> I'm very glad about all of me."

Many other nursery children have enjoyed singing this song since then. (See page 226.)

In one nursery class, children especially enjoyed rocking in their rocking boat. Often the teacher sang to a group of them as they rocked, using songs she had learned from the teacher's textbook. One day Margie Alice began to sing,

> "We are rocking, rocking, rocking,
> In our little boat,
> It is fun to go a-rocking,
> In our little boat."

The teacher and some of the other children joined her in this bit of song. Though that child has now been promoted to the kindergarten, other nursery children continue to enjoy singing Margie Alice's song.

> "Happy, happy, happy,
> Thank you, thank you, thank you, God,"

sang Elizabeth as she let the sand trickle through her fingers. Using Elizabeth's words with slight rearrangements the song, "When I'm Very Happy," was written and became a favorite with several nursery groups. (See page 223.)

As has been suggested before, desirable ways of acting may be suggested in song. Suggestions for moving quietly, for stacking blocks neatly, for picking up toys from the floor and putting them on shelves, for taking turns, for gathering for a time of rest, all are more pleasantly responded to if expressed musically. Appropriate tunes will be original with the leader.

Rhythmic Play

Children like to make music with blocks, sticks, drums, rattles, gourds, boxes filled with seed, bells, and anything else they can use for shaking, rattling, tapping, or beating to produce rhythm. While the wise nursery class leader will not subject children to the abnormal discipline of practices, rehearsals, and repetition called for by "Kiddie Bands," she may encourage the children in clapping their hands, tapping their feet, and using improvised instruments to keep time to the music of piano, record player, or the singing voice of the teacher.

A Record Player

Sometimes the mechanics of the record player are more interesting to children than music produced by it. Even so, they will enjoy hearing carols, quiet music, marches, and other music with strong rhythmic beat. No effort at interpretation, such as is used with older girls and boys is recommended. If some children wish to listen while others are engaged in noisy play, a worker may ask them to play quietly so as not to disturb the listeners. The listeners like to gather close to the record player, where they can watch as they listen.

As one group listened to Percy Grainger's "Country Gardens" the leader said, "The man who made this pretty music thought about flowers, green grass, birds, and butterflies." One little girl rose from the floor and began to skip. The teacher rose, too, joining hands with a child near her and they both moved about to the music. When they were seated again, the teacher said, "We moved like the flowers in the wind, didn't we?"

Some well-accented marches, and music with suggested rhythm like "Skater's Waltz" are good record selections. Many of the producers of records are providing simple forms of good music for children, but it is usually interpreted for older children. Care should be taken to help children learn to like good music. In this day of radio,

Photograph by Patty Chadwell

television, and jukebox, children are exposed to much that is raucous and cheap.

The *My Book* nursery album records are made from selections from the children's books. These records may be used at church school or at home. In churches where most of the children who come to church school go home at the end of the session and only a few remain during the church hour, use of these records for those who stay during the second hour may be valuable.

Dramatic Play

Dramatizing activities, such as galloping ponies with speed regulated by the piano or voice of the teacher, boats or trains chugging along, leaves falling down, trees swaying in the wind, birds and butterflies flying, are more fun if accompanied by good music. Sometimes such play may grow to dramatic play involving group thinking. The merry-go-round play and train play already described are two examples of such experiences. Sometimes a pleasing rhythm is set up, such as the sound of the train moving slowly with a chug-chug-chug, then faster and faster.

As children enjoy singing, listening, or moving to music, it should be kept in mind that this is done for their own pleasure and to provide them with opportunities for expression of emotion and expenditure of energy. They should not be urged to sing nicely nor to learn songs to share with others. It is unfair to young children to exploit them as "performers" for adult gratification. Sometimes young children will sing while adults are listening, but it should be informally, not for programs.

Nursery children are too young to be included in children's or "cherub" choirs. They are not yet ready for the practicing and performing of even simple music because they are not yet ready for the group discipline required for satisfactory results. With music, as with drawing and modeling, it is the happy development of the children with which the nursery class is concerned, not the production of a performance which is acceptable to adults.

IO

Use of Creative Art Materials

EVERY PERSON SHOULD BE ABLE TO EXPRESS HIMSELF THROUGH mediums other than the spoken word. Such mediums as music and other creative arts, as well as building materials, provide emotional outlets, relief from tensions, points of contact with other people. A sense of achievement which may come from the use of these mediums enriches personality and makes life better for those who understand, use, and enjoy them. It is not our purpose as teachers of three-year-olds to teach singing or painting. It is our purpose to provide opportunities for children to have experiences in association with groups of their peers through which they may develop wholesome personalities at a three-year-old level. Most of the learning experiences of nursery children will come through play, conversation, excursions, and so on. Since art materials usually call for a higher degree of co-ordination than the three-year-old has, only the occasional use of them in simple ways contributes to this experience.

From the first evidence of interest in color, or recognition of beauty, the young child's art experience begins. As he strings large beads or colored spools on a heavy string, fits the pieces together in a simple puzzle or puzzle-type toy, as he tears a blossom to pieces, he begins to get the feel of color, shape, and form. As the child experiments with a new material, smelling, tasting, feeling, manipulating, he begins to sense texture. Such opportunities to explore media should be part of the home experience of every child long before he is encouraged to use them as a means of expression or creation. Unfortunately, some children do not have these delightful experiences for experimentation at home. These experiences have value only when the child himself uses the medium.

Since the church nursery class is limited by time, by the clothing worn by some of the children, and other factors, use of such materials presents problems to teachers. Some decide that because of the difficulties, they will simply omit their use and hope that children will have experiences with them at home. Others, understanding that these materials are valuable for children, use them indiscriminately and find themselves facing many difficult situations. Still others plan carefully for occasional use of various types of art materials and discover ways of achieving good results through their use.

79

It would be unwise to list certain materials, saying some may be used successfully in all groups, while others should not be used until children are older. There are differences in situations, in numbers of children, and in the skill with which teachers are able to guide children. Some suggestions for use of various types of creative art materials with nursery class groups follow, with full realization that not all of these suggestions should be followed in any one group, but the leader will be selective.

Crayons

Perhaps the most commonly used (and abused) form of art activity for young children is "coloring." Too often they are given pictures in outline form, or color books and urged to stay within the lines as they color the pictures. Such practice discourages the creative tendencies of the child. Long before he is ready to use crayon or pencil as a means of producing his own idea of the way something looks, he is limited by the forms produced by those who are older and more skilled than he. Since he has not developed sufficient co-ordination of his muscles to stay skillfully within the lines, he is inclined to become either careless as he scribbles on the pictures or tense as he tries to do what is asked of him. Neither is desirable. If crayons are left where he may have free access to them, he is likely to use them for drawing in many undesirable places, such as walls, floor, and furnishings, and is likely to scatter the crayons to be stepped on.

Such materials may be made available only occasionally under the guidance of an adult. Short pieces of no-roll, large size crayons and big (about 12 by 14 inches) pieces of drawing paper should be provided. These may be enjoyed when used on the floor, at a table, or best of all at an easel. When a child stands to draw, he is likely to draw with big strokes, using his big muscles with no attempt to control his small muscles which are not ready yet for such use.

Often young children draw before they make a picture of something. Sometimes they will ask an adult to tell them what it is. Experimenting with materials precedes creative expression. Early art efforts should not be taken home lest they be laughed at or not understood by members of the family. If you wish to have children take something home, make up the card or booklet and let the child color it, put a seal on it, or slip a flower through a slit in it. Speak of it as something he can take to his family from "you and your teacher."

Clay

The young child who plays with clay should be permitted to enjoy the sensory satisfaction and relaxation of doing so, not urged to make something. Release from tension is its principle value. It is not wise for the teacher to make things for him to attempt to copy. Clay is helpful because it gives a child satisfactory occupation through which he may relax and forget himself. Some otherwise shy children will talk freely while their hands are busy. The fact that the dough may be divided many times makes it a means of bringing several children together in companionship. Its use provides many opportunities for the teacher to call children by name as she comments on how nice it is that friends may work together with clay. She may make up and sing to the tune of "Farmer in the Dell," some such songs as,

"It's fun to work with clay,
It's fun to work with clay,
It's fun to roll and mash and squeeze
It's fun to work with clay.

It's fun to work with John,
It's fun to work with Susan,
It's fun to work with all our friends,
In our own nursery class."

Some types of wallpaper cleaner, commercially prepared playdough or plasticine are clean and enjoyable for use as clay. A homemade mixture is quite satisfactory: Four cups of flour, one cup of salt, one tablespoon of salad oil, enough water to make a soft dough. Powdered tempera or vegetable coloring may be used. Sift flour and salt into a pan. Mix coloring with water and add gradually. Knead as you would bread dough until the mixture is smooth and easy to handle. The more it is kneaded, the smoother it becomes. This clay corrodes metal and becomes dry when not kept in sealed containers or plastic bags. Use of clay should be restricted to an oilcloth-covered table. The rug or floor covering must be protected.

Paints

If there is an expanded session, some of the older children may enjoy using paints. It is not recommended for the one-hour session.
Washable paints with big (half inch) camel's hair brushes and

large sheets of paper are a delight to young children. Paints are not recommended for use in most nursery classes since they must be carefully supervised to prevent clothing from being soiled. Even though the young painter wears an apron, he is likely to get paint on his clothing. Occasional use of paint during. a weekday gathering may be enjoyed. Finger painting is delightful but extremely mussy so is not recommended for Sunday sessions. It may be enjoyed during the week. In any situation where freedom of activity is not hampered by being dressed up, children enjoy experimenting with many varieties of art material.

A ten-cent paint brush and an empty can may provide the fun of imaginary painting. Some teachers have found that occasional use of this activity has provided happy, interesting activity for children who busily paint everything in sight and do no damage to clothing or equipment in the process.

Scissors

Young children like to cut paper. Unfortunately they often cut other things, even the lace from another's fancy pinafore. Therefore, scissors are not recommended for use in the church nursery class.

Wadding and Tearing Newspaper

Some teachers have found that highly emotional children get relief from pressure by tearing and wadding big pieces of newspaper. These may be tossed about, laughed at, and jammed into the waste basket. The child should understand that only papers kept in a designated place are to be so used. It is well to explain this use of paper to parents. Then the children may have a specially designated pile of newspaper for this use at home.

Pasting

Very rarely do nursery workers find it worthwhile to use paste in any form in the nursery class. When it is used, it is handled much as paint is and the sensory satisfaction from its use provides its greatest value. The functional use of paste is not significant to three-year-olds. Occasional licking, or moistening with a sponge or damp cloth, of seals to be pasted on cards may give children satisfaction. The value of paste at nursery level is so limited as to cause workers not to use it until children are older.

Care for Supplies

Creative art materials used in the nursery class should be kept in good condition, out of the children's reach, in a teacher's supply cabinet or closet. Crayons may be kept in baskets, boxes, or small pans. Paper should be cut and stacked so that it will not become mussed. Clay should be kept in plastic bags in covered crocks or jars or tightly sealed containers to prevent hardening.

Pieces of oilcloth or table tops which can be wiped clean with a damp cloth are needed for use with clay or paint. Even though children wear washable clothes and the materials used are of the kind which will wash out, protective aprons are desirable. These may be made from oilcloth or plastic.

While parents should be encouraged to dress their children sensibly in washable clothes, and some soiling of clothing is almost unavoidable, teachers should be reasonably careful not to allow children to be destructive of their own or other children's apparel. Such co-operation of parents and teachers is not difficult to achieve and is worthwhile if the two groups are to work together with understanding.

The use of some materials make hand washing necessary. Facilities for washing should be inside or adjacent to the classroom.

II

Special Occasions

NURSERY WORKERS SHOULD BE AWARE THAT NOTHING IS QUITE SO important to three-year-olds as happy, routine procedures. They will be careful to avoid the overstimulation of excessive celebration of special occasions. They will keep in mind that nursery class experiences are individual and take place in a small group, and that not every child will participate when there is a special emphasis. For instance, in one group, two or three children played birthday party throughout most of a morning session. They stirred up cake in the cooking pans, they set the table, they talked about parties. A teacher suggested that birthdays meant growing bigger and being able to do things to help. She told them a story and sang a song about this. When they sat down at the tea table, she said a prayer of thanks for growing and for birthdays. Other children in the same room during the same session did not enter into this activity and were not even aware of attention being paid to the birthday. The children were having experiences of equal value and importance to them in other activities.

In many churches children are promoted from the group for two-year-olds to the class for three's on the Sunday following the third birthday, hence entrance into the class is associated with the birthday. Workers in the two groups should keep one another informed, and an effort be made on the part of the teachers in the class for three-year-olds to become acquainted with the child before he enters the nursery class. Parents and teachers should help the child to feel that going to the new class is a desirable feature of being three.

Since big parties and crowds of any sort are overstimulating for young children they are not recommended. Neither is the use of candles, on either a real cake or an artificial cake, considered good for the nursery class. There should be recognition of the birthday, perhaps singing "Happy Birthday." There should be a brief prayer for the child on the Sunday nearest the birthday. "Thank you, God, for Stevie. We are glad he is growing bigger and stronger" or "We are glad that he is growing big enough to help at home and at church."

Most three-year-olds enjoy playing birthday in the housekeeping area and those who do not have a birthday at the time like pretending that they do. Teachers should know the date of each birthday, have

84

these recorded, and be able to mention the time when each child will have his birthday. Emphasis should be placed on growth and increase in the number of things which can be done as we grow. A birthday card, mailed to the child from his teachers, is welcomed since three-year-olds and four-year-olds like to receive mail.

Due to the increasing number of churches providing separate kindergarten groups for four-year-olds and five-year-olds, the practice of promoting children from the nursery class to the kindergarten on their fourth birthday is no longer recommended. Rather, at the beginning of the church-school year, those children who will enter the public school in two years, go from the nursery class into the church kindergarten. This means that teachers should check with local authorities to learn the date which is set for determining the age at which a child enters public school. This will mean that some children will remain in the nursery class for longer than one year while others will be there for less than one year.

Sometimes the child who is not promoted, because his or her fourth birthday comes a few days or weeks after the date fixed, seems more mature and more nearly ready for promotion than some of those who are within the age group. Some workers after consultation with parents and kindergarten workers have promoted such children. When this is done it is simply postponing the break. Since the child will not be permitted to enter public school early and since church-school curriculum is based upon public-school grade levels, most people believe that it is wiser to make the adjustment at the time of promotion from nursery to kindergarten rather than postponing it.

While kindergarten procedures aim to help the individual child as do nursery procedures, the greater degree of informality in nursery class is likely to mean that the individual is served as such. Hence, the children who are not promoted may be helped to rejoice that they will now be the biggest children in their class. They may help younger children who come in to learn to know and like the things done in nursery class. The older children may be privileged to enjoy more advanced activities, such as rhythmic play, more difficult puzzles, and perhaps work with clay.

In addition to becoming acquainted with the kindergarten teachers and room, some groups have found it wise to have one of the nursery workers go with the group for a few Sundays until they feel at home in the new situation.

The Promotion Day procedure should be kept as calm and happy as possible. It is not considered wise to have nursery children participate in any general program for an entire church school. Rather, when the children who are to enter the next group have left the four-year-old kindergarten, the teacher of that group should come to the nursery classroom and invite those who are to be promoted to go with her to their new room. Here they will be shown about the room, given their new books, *At Church and Home,* Part 1 (or *Kindergarten Lesson Pictures*).

Nursery-class workers may feel a bit of sadness at seeing these children whom they have come to know and love leave the nursery class. Mature workers will keep this emotion under control and join with the children in being proud that they have grown bigger and are ready to go to the kindergarten.

In preparing for Promotion Day, workers should plan for the best interest of the children. Care should be taken to avoid any display or showing off of children for the satisfaction of adults.

Certain religious occasions may be a part of the nursery class experience, but care will be taken that children are asked to share only in those celebrations for which their experience makes them ready. This will likely mean that things will go on very much as usual in the nursery class, with perhaps a bit of enrichment due to a special occasion, rather than big changes in procedure. As holidays approach teachers will do well to think together to determine the meaning of each celebration from the standpoint of the three-year-old and be prepared to answer questions or make comments which will be helpful.

Where promotion is a fall experience, Halloween is likely to be the first time of celebration for the nursery-class child. Certainly there will be no witches and black cats used in the room. Since very young children may have been taken in costume on "Trick or Treat" expeditions, and since some of them may have been frightened, teachers may have opportunities to mention that dressing up and playing games are fun, and otherwise encourage children to overcome any fears which may have begun through such experiences. The Halloween plans should be used the Sunday preceding Halloween.

Often the little child is frightened by Halloween celebrations of older children in the family or neighborhood. Part of the religious responsibility of the church-school leader is to build up a sense of security that will carry over into these everyday situations in the home life of the child. This is not to be interpreted as a time for dressing nursery children in grotesque costumes, but as one when an undergirding of security may save the little child from fright. The leader may decide to have a pumpkin cut with the features of a jack-o'-lantern. She will not use a lighted candle because of the danger of fire. It is better to have no light inside, for the little child gains an adequate sensory experience by touching the eyes and nose and mouth. He feels the whole pumpkin and may carry it around the room with him. The jack-o'-lantern is no longer strange and frightening. He knows what it is and how it is made.

Young children live in the here and now. History and historical celebrations are not meaningful to them. Thanksgiving, as a celebration of patriotic fervor, is not significant to them, nor is the Fourth of July. But, gratitude for food is of prime interest. Hence, the nursery class, during November, and at many other times during the year, will enjoy playing tea party, buying food, preparing it, and saying to God that we are glad for it. Playing picnic may be enjoyed in July and at other times. Mention that God plans for us to have food is wiser than saying that he gives it to us, since three-year-olds interpret literally all that they hear. It is difficult for them to understand how God gives us food, when they go with Mother and Father on the trip to the grocery store when it is bought, or say "thank you" to Grandmother or a friendly neighbor when some delicacy is brought in.

Most workers do not believe it wise to serve food weekly to young children who spend only one hour in the church school. If juice is to be served in the extended session, details should be cleared with parents in order that allergies may be avoided. If cookies or juice are served during every session there is danger that this repetition will cause church school to become "the place where we eat." This idea would supplant the joys of finding himself at home with a group of friendly children and adults within his church. Such loss of balance is unfortunate. Real food detracts from the pleasure of make-believe, too. With only pots, pans, dishes, and a stove, children can enjoy meat, vegetables, and dessert galore. There is also the feeling on the part of many parents that they would prefer that their children not be fed between meals because of all the individual differences regarding diet. A small serving of fruit or bread and butter during Thanksgiving month or for a summer picnic will not establish the habit of eating but may provide vivid experiences for giving thanks.

Very early in his life, in his home, and in the church school, the baby and the toddler live through Christmas experiences of beauty and reverence, which are associated with Jesus the Baby and his birthday. Unfortunately, many young children are confused by crowds in stores as they go with adults on shopping trips, too much food, too much noise, and too many new playthings at one time. While emphasizing the joy of Mary, Joseph, and others at the birth of Jesus, the happiness of sharing with others on his birthday, and the beauty of greens and decorations, nursery class teachers will try to maintain an atmosphere of secure enjoyment of doing the familiar things to which the child is accustomed.

Playing postman and receiving valentines because friends love us is fun which three-year-olds appreciate. The story behind the custom should be kept for later years.

A special need that arises in spring is the isolation of the children from the adult celebration of Easter. Those children who may have heard stories or seen pictures of the events preceding the first Easter may need special help to safeguard them from an emotional shock that may not have been evident to the persons who showed them the pictures. No mention of the Crucifixion or Resurrection either by name or description of what it means should ever be used with nursery children. Easter to adults is a day of rejoicing because of the risen Christ after the days when they have remembered his suffering.

For the little child there is a simpler, non-theological interpretation of the season. The leader may speak of the joy of Easter. She will try to stimulate happiness and a feeling of security because of the beauty of springtime and as a special time for remembering stories about Jesus. The interpretation of Easter for these three-year-olds will remain one of joyous celebration because of the return of spring, the growth of the seeds and flowers that they have planted, the opening up of tiny leaves, and the feeling that this is God's world. He has given us many things richly to enjoy.

The little child is not taken into the Easter service planned for adults or for older children. These experiences do not meet the religious need of little children for they only confuse and shock them.

Having guests in the home and taking trips are year-round experiences for most nursery children. During the summer vacation season, when such experiences are most common, play, stories, songs, and pictures may be used to help emphasize the pleasure. Nursery workers may give suggestions as to how young children may derive benefit from sharing in entertaining guests, as well as ways in which travel may be made more comfortable for them.

Each of these special occasions will be taken into account in preparation for Sunday-by-Sunday sessions as outlined in the guidance material for teachers and adults who direct the children at home and in the church nursery class.

12

The Vacation Church School
and the Three-Year-Old

SINCE VACATION CHURCH SCHOOLS ARE HELD IN MANY AREAS JUST
as soon as the public-school sessions end, we should perhaps look at
some of the questions which arise concerning three-year-olds and their
participation in these activities. Many people ask such questions as:
Should the nursery group for three-year-olds be included in the
vacation school? If not, why not? If so, what sort of preparation
should be made for them? Where can we get curriculum material?

Most thoughtful workers with three-year-olds are doubtful as to
the wisdom of including three-year-olds in vacation church schools.
Such experiences are likely to prove tiring and overstimulating for
such young children. If, after careful consideration the commission on
education of your church decides to have a nursery class in vacation
church school (often to provide for three-year-olds whose parents
teach in the vacation school) certain minimum requirements[1] should
be met:

1. Leadership. The choice of mature leaders who understand young
children is very important because they will be with the children for
several hours every morning. At least one well qualified leader should
be provided for each six children in the group and there must be a
minimum of two adults.

2. Enrollment. The number of children must be limited because
a large group is too stimulating for young children and the church
wants the experience to be a happy and satisfying one for the children.
It is they who will suffer if the rule is disregarded.

Churches can insist on advance enrollment, stating that the registra-
tion will be closed when the maximum of fifteen to eighteen is
reached.

3. Physical Environment and Equipment. Do we have available or
are we willing to secure needed space and equipment? There should
be provided thirty-five square feet of indoor play space per child
and an area for outdoor play that is safe and shaded so that children

---

[1] By Grace Storms. Excerpts from the article, "Planning for the Three-Year-Olds in the Vacation Church
School." From *Child Guidance in Christian Living*.

will not be exposed to the hot sun for too long a time and that need not be shared with older boys and girls. Since the children will be at the church each day for two hours or longer a room that may be darkened for resting and has accessible bathroom facilities is essential. The room needs to be clean, sunny, and attractive. It is wise to check state and community laws concerning such groups, and to have the advice of a local doctor.

The play equipment is the same as for any good nursery program.

Rest mats are needed for a rest period. Bath mats that are provided by the parents and marked with the child's name on one corner serve this purpose very well.

4. Program. The children in the nursery group should be protected from meetings with other groups. Joint sessions will have no value for them, and the natural restlessness of these young children when forced into experiences planned for older groups will be disturbing to the older children.

By all means, use your regular lesson material. Week after week and month after month there are more suggestions than any group can possibly carry out. Stories, songs, games, and activities from the material may be expanded, repeated, or used for the first time. In addition, many activities, such as painting, playing outdoors, hammering, and digging, may be a part of weekday activities which are not practical on Sunday. The freedom of dress and the longer session will permit activities which are not usually included in Sunday morning experiences.

Teachers who are mature enough and sufficiently well-trained to undertake to guide vacation church school sessions for three-year-olds will be able to find sufficient curriculum help in the regular lesson material.

PART TWO

A Year in the Nursery Class

FOR PERSONAL ENRICHMENT, A FEW SIMPLE SUGGESTIONS FOR teachers to use as Bible study are made in connection with the materials for each month. These are for adult enrichment and should not be shared directly with three-year-olds.

How to Use the Sunday-by-Sunday Plans

In the pages which follow, some suggestions are given for Sunday-by-Sunday procedures in the class for three-year-olds. Each group of teachers who use them will find that it is necessary to adapt them in accordance with space, numbers of children, and equipment available.

Since learning is an individual experience at three, and since teaching is done on that basis, the suggestion will be used with one or a few children at a time. It is not recommended that all children be gathered together to hear a story, to pray, or to sing during the session. Some workers have a struggle with themselves because they fear that unless they do bring the children together they are not teaching. They should recognize that teaching and telling are not the same thing. The child who is happy playing with puzzles or trains may go home with a satisfied sense that his church is a happy place. If so, he has "learned" and a basic foundation for a Christian philosophy of life has been established. It is not essential that he hear or say words which express this learning. As the child grows, becomes accustomed to the activities in the room, and learns that the suggestions made by the teachers are interesting and helpful, he will join more readily in group activity. Even then, since the young child lives in the here and now, he should not leave one activity in which he is interested in order to share in another just because the other includes more listening or was planned for this session. This does not mean that children run wild, unsupervised and with no enriching suggestions from teachers. Rather, every person in the room is alert for every opportunity to help the children. This may be through use of words, or it may be by simply being near to be helpful when needed. Learning when to speak and when to leave children alone is a difficult skill. Informal teaching does not mean chaos. It demands careful study and preparation. Informal teaching in the nursery class is that way of working with three-year-olds in which the teacher follows the suggestion of the child and is ready to interpret religiously the experiences that arise.

The suggestions for one Sunday may be more usable on another. Some will be repeated because they are found to be helpful with your group of children. Some you will try and, failing to get a satisfactory response from the child or children in your group, you will abandon. Some of these may prove useful at another time.

One young teacher told of planning for a picnic in July. She tried throughout the month to interest the children in playing picnic. There was not enough interest in her suggestions to merit her continuing with them. At Thanksgiving time, a great deal of interest was evidenced in playing that a big dinner was to be prepared and served in the housekeeping center. One energetic, dominating child insisted that everyone in the room should come to dinner at the same time. There was not enough room at the table, nor enough chairs for all. The young teacher, recalling her plans for July, suggested that table cloths and sheets from the doll bed be spread over some big blocks and that the group sit around them on the floor. They had a Thanksgiving picnic. While the children heard a prayer of thanks for good food and good friends, the teacher said she prayed, inwardly, a prayer of thanksgiving for preparations made in July which stood her in good stead in November.

The session plans which follow are built around common experiences of three-year-olds and the purposes of Christian education for them. These plans are grouped together somewhat loosely, not as the more formal units planned for older children. Some of these interests will be ongoing so that pictures, stories, songs, and activities suggested for one session may be used during another. Some special emphasis may continue over a period of several weeks.

Each group of workers should plan carefully for each session and for several sessions ahead. Materials which will enrich the emphasis chosen, should be provided and brought to the children's attention. Other materials, such as pictures, books, creative art materials, and so on, which would likely divert the attention of the children, should be put away in the teacher's supply cabinet. If there is a real need for them, they can be brought out for use.

Every teacher should be familiar with the material in the teacher's text and the pupils' books and should recognize that every adult in the room is a teacher. No one person is *the* teacher, with others just helping.

Workers should accept the fact that not all children will have the same experiences each Sunday. It is not necessary that every child shall hear the same story, song, or prayer, or engage in the same play. By careful planning, knowing materials which will enrich their efforts, studying each child, and endeavoring to meet his needs, it is reasonable to expect that during a year in the nursery class, each child will hear some stories, songs, and prayers. He will enjoy individual and group activities of his own choosing and at the suggestion of adults. He will enter the four-year-old kindergarten with certain evidences of development. These are summarized in the goals for Christian education for three-year-olds, as outlined by the Curriculum Committee of The Methodist Church and discussed in Chapter One of this book, beginning on page 9.

Some experiences through which these goals may be accomplished are:

• Early contacts with the church through visitors in home; parents' attendance at church.

• Play, individual and in groups of two and three children.

• Sentence-length prayers.

• A few carefully selected stories from the New Testament.

• Looking at and talking about the Bible.

• Recommended songs and pictures.

• Dramatic play, stories, conversation, to interpret conduct patterns and lead to fellowship.

• Joyous participation in small group activities in nursery class.

Planning for the Year

The plans in this book begin with the fall quarter, starting with the first Sunday in October. This material is planned for church schools which have a separate class for three-year-olds. The year in the nursery class begins for John when he enters, not on a fixed date. Some children will spend less than a year. Others will stay several months after their fourth birthday. Promotion to kindergarten will be on Promotion Day two years before the child will enter first grade in school.

Teachers will need to be alert to meet the needs of the youngest children in the group, while supplying more activities and enrichment for those who are four, nearly four, or even four-and-a-half.

This is another reason in favor of individual and small group rather than large group teaching.

In order to be helpful, especially to untrained, inexperienced workers, specific suggestions are given for some use of materials and activities. Throughout the session plans, specific suggestions are given for procedure in some interest centers, and for carrying out some activities. It is hoped that these may be useful as suggestions for other activities. In each month's plans, some detailed suggestions will be given and a list of other activities included.

The emphasis during the year will center around family life, neighborhood experiences, transportation, sources of foodstuff, wonders of nature, the fellowship of church life, God's plan for his children, and about Jesus as a baby, as a little boy, and as a man who grew up to be good and kind and taught people about God. Through pictures, stories, songs, prayers, and planned activities, some of these will be emphasized strongly at one time, others at another. Some of them will run like a thread of bright color throughout the year's pattern.

FALL QUARTER

October

POSSIBLE MATERIALS AND ACTIVITIES

Possible Stories for October (select from *My Book for Fall*, Part 1): "Come to Church," "Friends at Church," "Autumn Leaves," "At the Market," "Autumn Leaves and Fruit."

Possible Songs for October: "Church Bells," "Church," "Friends at Church," "Leaves Are Falling."

Possible Pictures for October: "Come to Church" from *Nursery Class Pictures.* See also page 98.

Possible Activities for October: Get acquainted walks around room. Doll play; block building; ball rolling. Look at books and pictures. Sing. Take trip outdoors to see autumn foliage and plant bulbs. Play with autumn leaves. Play with jack-o-lantern.

My Picture Card: Select from October, November, December.

DURING OCTOBER, NURSERY CLASS TEACHERS SHOULD VISIT IN THE homes of their pupils, if possible, coming to know the child and his family. *My Book for Fall* may be shown and explained to the parents on this visit, pointing out materials planned especially for them. During the visit the worker should learn to know the child and be known by him and should share with the parents a general idea of the goals and procedures of the nursery class. Throughout the year, when a new child enters the nursery class, a worker should call on him in his home. It is best that this precede his coming to the class so that he is welcomed by an adult friend. If this is not possible, the visit should be made during the week following his entry into the group. Be sure that each child enrolled in the three-year-old nursery class in October be three years from entering first grade of public school.

Purpose

To help the children establish happy relationships with the church, including a sense of belonging; to think of the church as a place where they have happy times with adult friends and friends their own age.

Suggested Bible Study for Teachers

Memorize Psalms 84. This is for your own enrichment, not for sharing with three-year-olds. Consider how much the church has enriched your life as you read, reread, and learn the Psalm. Share it at your planning meeting with others who work with you in the nursery class.

Preparations for October Sessions

Read suggestions for the entire month, pages 95 to 106.

Secure name tags and have one ready for each child, with extra ones available. (See page 50.)

Read "Halloween," page 105, and secure necessary materials.

Have ready an offering container.

Provide a housekeeping center, including several cuddly dolls.

Place some soft toys and some floor toys, such as an interlocking floor train to invite floor play.

Provide large hollow blocks and smaller blocks for building.

Have a truck or wagon (this may be a box with casters and a rope for pulling) for hauling blocks.

Provide a few small, empty cans, food cartons, and pictures of food mounted on cardboard.

A basket and some paper bags may be used by small shoppers.

Provide a cart, wagon, or large truck for delivering food.

Cut from magazines pictures of food, fruit, and milk to be placed on the picture rail, or made into a book for the book table. Include a picture of people saying thanks to God.

Provide a place for displaying pictures and select those showing children at play in nursery class and families going to church; of fruits and vegetables at store or market; autumn leaves or children playing in leaves.

Have selected books available which will provide opportunities for conversation and sentence stories about the church.

Provide a glass jar and a sweet potato for planting.

On a window sill, shelf, or table, keep seasonal nature objects such as colored leaves, seed pods, acorns, and berries. Be sure that these are fresh and attractive each Sunday. Have magnifying glass available.

Provide simple puzzles. Try to secure one of a bus or automobile.

Provide a large ball for rolling.

Secure bulbs and have small garden space dug up for planting bulbs.

Have picture of a tulip, jonquil, crocus, or whatever bulb is planted.

Provide a box of leaves.

Have at least one piece of big muscle equipment and outdoor play equipment if possible.

Piano and/or record player, or a box with a keyboard painted on it may be a "music center." Songs may be mounted on cards for the children to use as they "play" the piano, or for the convenience of the new pianist who may not be familiar with all of the songs.

Before each session, check the room carefully to be sure that workers are ready to help three-year-olds have experiences there which will contribute to accomplishing the purpose you have in mind. Most important, plan to spend time in thoughtful preparation for the responsibility that you have accepted, and in prayer that God may grant you the patience and wisdom to teach three-year-olds.

Stories and Songs for Use in October

Since some of the children in the class may be barely three, new to the group, and unaccustomed to having stories told or read to them, stories may be only one or two sentences long during this month. Each teacher should be familiar with all of the stories in *My Book for Fall,* suggested for use in October. (See page 95.) The stories should be learned well enough for the idea in each to be shared in conversation at any time during the month with one or several children.

Several copies of *My Book for Fall* should be available in different parts of the room. Each teacher should take advantage of any opportunity which presents itself to use them with individuals or with small groups of children. The older children will be more likely to wish to have one or several stories each Sunday. Stories may be enjoyed at the table where nature objects are on display, near a picture, at the book center, or on the floor with children who are playing. The story about the leaves should be used when the foliage in your area is at such a stage as to make the experience described in it meaningful. It is not "the lesson" on a given Sunday. Like the other stories, it may be used often. As stories are told, remind the children that these same stories are in the book they have to enjoy at home. (Resourceful teachers in parts of the country where leaves do not change color on trees, find brilliant colors in leaves of some plants and bushes.)

All workers should learn the songs and should be prepared to share them at any time that they fit in with the conversation or activities, either with individuals or with groups.

Pictures for Use in October

Pictures may be selected from the set, *Nursery Class Pictures*. Others, clipped from a copy of *My Book for Fall* and from magazines, may be mounted. All should be ready for use. Placed on the picture rail, screen, or table they provide interest for individual children and often induce conversation.

SUGGESTED PROCEDURE

(While the procedure suggested for one Sunday may well be used on another, for convenience in planning, we are suggesting Sunday-by-Sunday plans.)

FIRST SUNDAY

As the children arrive, they should be greeted and encouraged to remove and hang their own wraps. Older children can do much for themselves, but those just three will need help and encouragement. A word or note to parents, asking that they permit teachers to give this help may be wise. Such a shared experience is good for helping the child learn to think of the teacher as his grown-up friend at church.

Each child will be given a name tag to wear and invited to walk around the room. On this walk, places of interest, such as books and housekeeping centers, may be pointed out. The offering container may be discovered and the explanation given, "This is where we put our money every Sunday. Our money helps to pay for our books and our electric light bill and to pay the persons who keep our room clean."

If a child clings to the member of his family who brings him, that person should be invited to remain in the room for a while, quietly seated on a small chair in an inconspicuous place. The child should be invited to participate and sooner or later will leave the person to enter into child activity. Only occasionally does a child need the person to stay with him more than a few minutes.

As a teacher walks with a child around the room she may call attention to pictures, books, and toys, saying, "These are for you to play with." She may pick up and offer to a timid, hesitant child a soft toy, a doll, or a block, suggesting something that may be done with it.

It is important that the children be taken into the rest room so that they may know where they will be taken when they wish to go to the toilet. In no case will there be more than two or three children in any one group who take this walk of discovery around the room.

As children become interested in activities or other children, teachers should leave them to their own devices. They should watch for evidences of restlessness, boredom, or unhappiness and make suggestions where they are needed.

From time to time teachers should mention the name of the child and of other children, expressing gladness for friends at church. For example, "I like a church where Tommy, Mary, and Bill can play with blocks together. I am going to sing a song about Mrs. (use her own name), Tommy, Mary, and Bill." Sing (see page 214),

> "Thank you, God, this happy day
> For friends at church who sing and play."

This may be done with any activity. A teacher and one or two children may play rolling the ball, calling the name of the children and the teacher often. Explain that the balls are always *rolled* indoors. We may throw or bounce balls when outdoors. Indoors, we roll balls.

Children in the housekeeping center may be encouraged to play taking their dolls to church or preparing dinner after church. Blocks may be used to make a street or sidewalk along which to walk.

If children are building aimlessly, a teacher may pick up a triangular block, place it on top of a pile of blocks and say, "This looks like a church now, David." This may provide an opening for a song, a story, or a prayer. The story, "Come to Church," *My Book for Fall*, page 5, may be used. But children should not be forced to abandon their own activities to listen.

At the book table, mounted pictures of homes, churches, and families going to church should provide opportunities for conversation. Children are glad to tell such things as, how they came to the church and with whom and to talk about their clothing. Show and talk about the large picture, "Come to Church."

Throughout the session, teachers will be alert to opportunities for prayer. "Thank you, God, for friends at church," or "We are glad that we may come to our church. Thank you, God," or a similar brief prayer may be used.

Two or three workers will be near the wrap rack to assist the children as parents arrive, in finding their own wraps and encouraging them in self-help. As the children go home, name tags should be taken off for use next Sunday. One of the church songs may be sung to the children as they leave if there is not too much confusion. At least one of the teachers should be alert to help the child whose parents do not come early, to remain happy and busy and not to feel forgotten. As each child leaves, give him *My Picture Card*, Number 1.

After the Session

Did the room seem to arouse the interest of the children? What evidence had you that this was a happy session? In what ways will you seek to be better prepared next session? What in your session was obviously religious?

SECOND SUNDAY

As the children arrive, encourage them to remove and hang their wraps. Some of them will go immediately to a center of interest which they recall and wish to enjoy again. During the session, seek in some way to call their attention to pictures and books about the church. This may be done in connection with their play. At a time when their interest seems to lag, or as a means of diverting attention when difficulties arise between the children as they play, you may invite them to go with you to see something pretty or interesting elsewhere in the room.

Ask the shy child to walk around with you, calling attention to interesting things in the room and mentioning your pleasure in having him there and your gladness for a church which provides a place for each of us to be happy. You may wish to tell the story, "Friends at Church," *My Book for Fall*, page 8, and call attention to pictures of children playing in nursery class and families going to church.

However, you may not tell a story. Often playing and talking together may be of far greater value than telling a story. If the story is told, it may be told to one child at the doll center, told again to two or three children at the block center, told again as a child and teacher look at a book or picture. The children will not be brought together in a group for a story.

If you have secured a puzzle of a bus or an automobile, the children will enjoy putting it together. Talk about the ways families come to church as the child works the puzzle.

Puzzles for the younger children should have not more than five or six pieces. In choosing puzzles, select very simple ones. If those available have too many pieces, you may use rubber cement to glue several parts to the board. By the time these work loose, children will probably have learned to put them together rapidly enough to utilize the larger number of pieces. The picture made by completing the puzzle will have meaning when you call attention to it. Some three-year-olds work puzzles easily and quickly. Others who are not accustomed to them will not be interested. Avoid talking to children too much when they are happy and busy playing with one another. But listen as they begin to talk to one another.

In the housekeeping area, you may wish to share a tea party. You may mention that it is a good Sunday dinner. Many families eat out on Sunday and children are glad to tell of family plans. You may say a prayer of thanks for the good dinner, for church, and for happy times together. You may show a picture or tell a story to the group at the table, but avoid dominating the group. If the children play happily without adult interference, permit them to do so.

One or two children at a time may wish to sit on the piano bench with the musician as she plays and sings the songs about the church. She may play with one hand, using the melody only, pronouncing the words plainly so that children will hear them. If the songs are clipped from one set of pupils' books and mounted on cards with pictures, it will help the children to know what the song is about. If there is no piano, the song cards, or book, may be placed on a rack fastened to a box upon which a keyboard has been painted. Children enjoy playing and singing with such a piano.

Repeat the ball-rolling game used last Sunday to help the children learn one another's names.

If there is an outdoor playground, the children who have been in the nursery class for several months may enjoy going outside to play. Some of these children and the new members of the group may prefer to stay in the room. There should be enough workers to make this possible. Especially is it unwise to rush the child who has not yet become accustomed to the room and the things in it. New experiences, such as going outdoors or to a different part of the building may be enjoyed later. Remember, each child should be permitted to develop at his own tempo.

As parents come for their children, sing one of the church songs, and comment that we are glad for our church. Name tags should be taken off and left for next Sunday, and *My Picture Card*, Number 2, given each child. Workers may help with wraps as in the last session.

THIRD SUNDAY

When the children come, greet them. When wraps have been removed and hung, put on name tags and follow the same procedure as on the two previous Sundays. If foliage in your area is turning, due to changes in fall weather, arrange bright-colored leaves, pictures of fall scenes, acorns, seed pods, and so on for the children to enjoy. Use these for several Sundays at the time of year when changes are taking place in your area. Such things are not significant to children unless they are a part of their experience. This may be during September, October, or even as late as November in some parts of the country.

If there are trees or bushes with brilliant foliage on the church lawn or in a yard nearby, make arrangements to take small groups of two or three children at a time to see this colored foliage. Such an experience should lead to a prayer, "Thank you, God, for the beautiful colors in leaves."

In a city church where outdoor experience with leaves is not possible, the teachers may bring in bags full of leaves for the children to enjoy. If kept in a cool place and not dried out, the leaves may be used for two Sundays. Teachers in Florida and Southern California have discovered brilliant foliage, hanging moss, and seed pods that have been substituted for the brilliant autumn leaves of the north.

In areas where there is little seasonal change evidenced in foliage, find seed pods, dried grass, hanging moss, and other evidences of maturity in plant life to share with children. A milkweed pod, broken open to release the seeds with wings, can provide interest and wonder. Three-year-olds will enjoy feeling the soft texture, watching them float when dropped or blown about, and hearing that many seeds are planted this way. A magnifying glass will add to the interest.

A sweet potato may be planted in a jar of water. If fall flowers or colored leaves are available, children may enjoy putting a few of these in a bowl or vase on the tea table. Elaborate arrangements are not desirable for the nursery class, as young children should be permitted to handle and explore. A box of leaves may be enjoyed as they are tossed about, scuffled through, gathered up and returned to the box.

If leaves are enjoyed during this session, the story, "Autumn Leaves," *My Book for Fall,* page 13, may be told. Otherwise one of the stories about the church may be used if a story is needed for this session.

If there is an outdoor play space, the children may enjoy filling a wagon with leaves and hauling it to be dumped in another part of the play yard. If there is no such place, perhaps a few of the children will enjoy taking a walk with one or more of the workers. If so, they may enjoy finding signs of fall to talk about, or leaves to pick up and bring back to the room. This will depend upon the situation of the church. If going outside does not seem wise, perhaps a tree, vine, or shrub outside the window may be enjoyed from inside. Or the leaves that have been brought by the workers may be enjoyed.

The song, "Leaves Are Falling," page 215, may be sung, followed by the prayer, "Dear God, we are glad for our beautiful world and that you planned for leaves to be pretty in the fall."

While waiting for parents, the children may sing and play "Leaves Are Falling." (See pages 207 and 215.)

As the children go home, you may wish to give each of them one pretty colored leaf, or an acorn, to show to their parents. *My Picture Card,* Number 3, may be given each child.

FOURTH SUNDAY

Greet children as usual. Since the weather is likely to be quite cool, new sweaters, coats, and other fall clothing will be worn. Comment on these. Hangers should be held and help given to children in removing and hanging their wraps.

If there is some special item of interest, such as colored leaves, or some new pictures, you may wish to call attention to these as children arrive. If some children go immediately to something in which they are interested, seek an opportunity to share it with them later in the session.

Sing the songs about the church and the leaves.

Use the picture and story, "At the Market," *My Book for Fall,* page 16.

Encourage conversation about going with Mother to buy food. There will be descriptions of helpfulness as the cart is pushed. Let children pick out vegetables and fruit shown in the picture and mention the colors.

Play grocery store. Put the groceries away when you get home to the play center. Keep in mind that filling and emptying paper bags, baskets, or boxes, loading and unloading a wagon or a truck, are fun in themselves. Do not become discouraged if the three-year-old is absorbed in the mechanics of the operation rather than in its dramatic possibilities.

In addition to *My Book for Fall,* mounted pictures of autumn scenes, and other picture books, may be used. A box of mounted pictures of fall and one of church will be enjoyed.

Show a bulb to a few children at a time. Explain that if we plant it carefully, after a long time, we will probably have a beautiful flower like the picture.

Take a few children at a time outside to plant the bulbs. Let those who wish, each plant one bulb. Show the children how to push the dirt over the bulb. You may explain, "We cannot make the bulb grow. But we can help. We put it in the ground and cover it carefully. There will be sunshine and rain and snow. A long time after Christmas, some morning we will find a beautiful flower where we planted a bulb." Pause, then pray, "Thank you, God, for bulbs and flowers. We are glad that we may plant bulbs. Thank you for rain and sunshine (include snow if you have snow in your section of the country) that help bulbs grow. Amen."

A few children may enjoy hearing the record about the church from the *My Book* Nursery album. In the housekeeping area, children may enjoy playing getting ready for church.

You may wish to show the children the Bible, saying, "When fathers and mothers sit in church, our minister reads to them from the Bible. It is a very special book." Or, you may use this opportunity for a story, a song, or a prayer.

Big muscle activity is necessary for comfort and happiness of the three-year-old. Something upon which he can climb should be provided. This may be a large set of parallel ladders, if space permits; an indoor slide, or a rocking boat, which when turned over provides steps and a space from which to jump. A very low bench, or walking board, or a set of steps may also be used for jumping. A teacher should be nearby when such equipment is in use to prevent accidents and to encourage the child who wishes to climb, or jump, but is fearful. Self-confidence and pleasure in company with other children are the desirable features of such activity. "Taking turns" becomes a part of the play in time, but three-year-olds are immature. We should not expect them to remember about turns without reminders.

As the children leave, call attention to the picture they are taking home today on *My Picture Card*, Number 4. Mention each child by name and tell him to be sure to tell Mother and Daddy about the fun we had (with leaves, planting bulbs, building with blocks, or whatever was the special interest of that child).

FIFTH SUNDAY (Or First Sunday in November)

If there is a fifth Sunday in October, continue with the emphasis on changes in the world about us due to the fall season. Use the picture of the mother and child arranging leaves and tell the story, "Autumn Leaves and Fruit," *My Book for Fall*, page 20. This may give opportunity for a brief prayer.

Enjoy the song and game, "Leaves Are Falling," page 215.

Activities at interest centers may be enjoyed as on previous Sundays.

My Picture Card, Number 5, will be given to the children.

Halloween

Halloween will come on the last day of October. The Halloween plans should be used the Sunday preceding Halloween. Workers with young children feel that three-year-olds should not participate in activities as "Trick or Treat" or UNICEF collections. But many of the children will hear older brothers and sisters discussing participation in such events. Some of the nursery children will be eager to tell of things they have seen or done. Some of them may enjoy this occasion. Others may be frightened and need reassurance.

Part of the religious responsibility of the church-school leader is to build up a sense of security that will carry over into these everyday situations in the home life of the child.

Any available pictures of Halloween fun will be mounted and placed on the screen or dado. Probably the leader will tell no story this Sunday, but plan for running conversation with one or two children at a time. The children may be encouraged to tell of plans they have heard older children talking about, of the "funny faces" they have seen in the store windows, or of the suits or dresses they have seen being made for the older children. The leader will encourage them to talk about how funny different ones look when they put on the faces, and what good times children can have with jack-'o-lanterns.

In this way the children may become accustomed to the idea of Halloween and fear that is often aroused may be avoided. It can be explained that the older girls and boys are really trying to make each other happy by dressing up and they would like to make little children happy, too, and so they plan a surprise and come to the house. "Thank you, God, for friends who want to make us happy," might be the prayer that is used this Sunday.

You may add a bit of reassurance by having a jack-o'-lantern to be looked at, touched, smelled, and carried around. No lighted candle will be used because of the danger of fire. But you may comment, "When a light shines through a jack-o'-lantern's funny eyes, nose, and mouth, people can see it at night. A jack-'o-lantern at a house tells everyone who sees it that friendly people live in this house."

Adjusting Your Plans

Be sure to plan for the entire quarter. If either October or November has five Sundays, arrange your sessions to have the Thanksgiving emphasis come the Sunday preceding Thanksgiving. If December is the f.ve-Sunday month, adjust your plans so that the Christmas plans will be used on the Sunday before Christmas. You may also need to readjust use of *My Picture Card*.

After the Session

As you recall the sessions of this month, what evidence is there that the children have adjusted to the situation without the "fours"? What have you done that was obviously religious? In what ways have you grown as a better nursery class teacher?

November

AS PART OF YOUR PREPARATIONS FOR NOVEMBER, BE SURE THAT your room is clean and in order. The teacher's supply closet or cabinet should be neat and any broken or worn toys repaired or replaced. Some new cooking toys may be needed, such as a small wooden salad bowl, to be used with a serving spoon, as a mixing bowl or a miniature roasting pan. Dish towels and small aprons will make this area more attractive.

Purpose

To nurture appreciation for good times in the family and a beginning understanding of God's plan that his children shall have food to enjoy and to nourish them; to continue to enjoy beauties of nature in autumn.

Suggested Bible Study for Teachers

Read for your own enrichment and to enhance your appreciation for the bounteous goodness of God: Genesis 1:29; Psalms 67, 98, 100, and 148. Participate in the adult worship services of Thanksgiving. Recount the many evidences of God's love and care for you. If you are truly thankful to God, the Creator and the giver of good gifts, you will be able to help boys and girls enjoy thinking together about families, food, and the beauty of the earth.

Preparation for November Sessions

Read suggestions for the entire month, pages 107 to 114.
Make the housekeeping area as attractive as possible.
Add new toys and equipment as needed.
Provide a short plank.
Provide books and magazine pictures showing farm animals and food; families having happy times together, fathers reading to children; families having grace at mealtime.
Have a box of paper napkins and some paper towels available.
Have ready small pieces of bread and butter for the second Sunday and a red, a yellow, and a ripe green apple, with a large paper bag for the third Sunday. A peeling knife will be needed also.
After reading the suggestions for all of November, reread the goals and purposes for nursery class teaching as listed on pages 7-12. How many of these goals do you hope to include this month?
In preparation for the third Sunday, notes should be written explaining any special Thanksgiving plans. Small safety pins will be needed for pinning on notes.
Three-year-olds should never be burdened with knowledge of the need and sufferings of others. Usually it is better not to ask them to bring gifts of food for charity. If they are to participate in a church-wide project of this sort, mention in your notes to parents that children are to bring a gift of some canned food, or of fresh fruit, to be shared with a friend because of friendship, not pity.
Provide a box or basket for gifts brought by the children.
If Thanksgiving precedes the fourth Sunday, adjust your sessions accordingly.

Stories and Songs

Adults may tire of constant repetition of the same story or song, but the little child welcomes the familiar. He enjoys hearing the same song and the same story over and over again. "Sing it to me again." "Tell it to me," the child requests as he brings pictures or a favorite picture book. He wishes the story told in the same way the fiftieth time as it was told him the first time. For this reason the leader repeats the same story several Sundays in succession instead of telling a new story each Sunday. There may be one familiar story told to a group of two or three children and a different familiar story told to another group of three or four children. When the child hears a story in the church school that Mother has read to him at home there is a familiar link between home and church.

SUGGESTED PROCEDURE

FIRST SUNDAY

If you do not have permanent name tags which you use throughout the year, you may provide name tags shaped like apples for use during November. These may be cut from red and yellow cardboard. As the children arrive, encourage them to help themselves in removing wraps. If money is brought as an offering, it should be placed in a basket or other container. You may comment, "We use the money we bring to pay for keeping our church warm and clean." Or you may say, "This money pays for things we use in our church." If this is repeated many times, children will not get the mistaken idea that they give the money to the teacher.

When children have disposed of their wraps and offering, they may go immediately to some activity in which they are interested. Sometimes a child comes in eager to talk and needs a sympathetic listener. In the rush of getting off on Sunday mornings, few families have an adult member who is free to listen. Some three-year-olds talk quite plainly, others are difficult to understand. If you will sit or stoop down to his level, and listen carefully, you may learn to understand the child who does not speak plainly. While it is all right to ask a child to repeat occasionally, you need to be careful in your response to the child whose speech is difficult to understand. You may smile, tell him you are not sure just what he said, and thank him for telling you. Remember that when you speak hurriedly, indistinctly, and without his full attention, he does not understand you, either. When talking with him, speak slowly, enunciate carefully, using simple terms. Give him time to think of what you say.

After the informal conversation, suggest an interesting activity at housekeeping, block, or book center, or near the piano to enjoy music, song or games. Sing "Friends at Church," page 214, and "Friends, Friends, Friends," (tune "Church" page 224).

Play cooking, eating, and doing the dishes. Show a picture of a family eating and saying grace. As a part of such dramatic play, there may be a simple prayer of thanks for food, for families, or for happy times of working together. Here again, do not insist that the cook stop cooking, or the delivery boy sit down if he prefers to continue to load and unload his truck, or that everyone stay at the table the same length of time, or that all of the children have this experience.

At the book table, or on a rug, enjoy pictures of food and of families having happy times together, fathers reading to children and so on. This may lead to telling the story, "Fun With Books," *My Book for Fall*, page 25. Use the picture, "In Nursery Class."

Let the children tell about times of reading at home, possibly at bedtime with grandparents or parents.

Play the game of growing from eating good food, using the words,

> "Now, I'm very, very small,
> I'll drink milk and grow up tall."

Stoop down as low as possible, play that you eat or drink the food or beverage mentioned and stretch tall with arms overhead. This game may be played with one or several children.

If weather permits in your section of the country, and there is outdoor play space available, those children who wish to do so should spend some time outdoors. If bulbs were planted they may be watered. As you go and come, and while on the playground, watch for opportunities to call children's attention to evidences that winter is coming or has come, such as bare limbs, leaves on the ground, berries, or acorns.

As parents call for their children, give any necessary assistance with wraps. Say to each child as he leaves, "We had a happy time together. I like our church, don't you? Be sure to tell Mother about the picture you take home today." (*My Picture Card*, Number 6.)

SECOND SUNDAY

(If Thanksgiving precedes suggestions for the fourth Sunday, adjust your plans to suit.)

As children arrive, there may be opportunity to comment on their warm clothing. If a child is wearing a coat left from last year or handed down from an older child, comment that we're glad our mothers take good care of our winter clothes for us; or glad that we have big brothers or friends who have outgrown sweaters that we can wear. Be sure to compliment each child. Avoid insincerity and help each child discover true cause for pleasure in what is his. Repeat last Sunday's suggested procedure concerning removing wraps, and putting offering into container.

Repeat any activities used last Sunday in which the children seem interested.

On the picture rail or board, have a row of mounted pictures of good food to eat. Be sure that the pictures are on the eye level of the children. Be careful to choose those foods that we wish to encourage three-year-olds to eat. Have several pictures of families enjoying a meal together and at least one of the family saying grace. Try during the session to have each child look at, talk about, and hear some comment on these pictures. A truck driver may be asked to drive his truck past the row of pictures and park it in a garage to be greased while he sees and hears about the pictures. Housekeepers may be invited to take their dolls to see the pictures. Other children may respond to the suggestion, "Let's look at these pictures together."

After the children have played for a short time the leader may go from group to group and suggest that she has a surprise. Perhaps they would like to put away their blocks or their toys or bring their dolls with them and come over by the piano. It is not necessary that all the children stop their play to come. If some show no interest in the invitation, the leader will not urge them. Any children who are interested will go over to the piano with her. If none of the children show any interest in the leader's invitation, she will go quietly to the piano and will sit on one of the small chairs and begin to unwrap the package of bread and butter.

Another leader will be ready to pass the paper napkins. Talk about the good bread and butter. Before eating, the leader may say, "I am going to close my eyes. We do not have to close our eyes when we talk to God but I like to. You may do as you wish." As she closes her eyes most of the children in the group will follow her example. "Thank you, God, for good bread and butter" or "We do like good bread and butter. Thank you, God" may be the prayer that is offered, or the leader may say, "I know a thank-you song," and then sing "Church," page 224, substituting the word "bread."

Sing the song, "Friends at Church," page 214.

If a new story is advisable, tell "A Happy Day," *My Book for Fall*, page 28, or "We Give Thanks," *My Book for Fall*, page 33. Or "Autumn Leaves and Fruit," *My Book for Fall*, page 20, may be retold.

Following the story, speak about the fun of playing together with friends at church, putting puzzles together, and so on. At the close of this conversation, suggest that the children go to work on puzzles, back to the housekeeping center, to the blocks, or to other interest centers. You may use the picture, "In Nursery Class."

As the children leave, be sure each has *My Picture Card*, Number 7.

THIRD SUNDAY

Greet the children as they arrive, help them with their wraps, mention some of the things for which the church uses their money and help each child to find something to do which interests him. As the children play singly or in small groups, move about among them with a paper bag containing three apples, one red, one yellow, and one green.

The suggestion to a few of the children that there is another surprise today will probably mean that the majority of the group will gather close to the leader as she brings out the paper bag with the apples in it. She will hold the bag together at the top with the opening arranged so that the children may slip in their hands but not see what is in the bag.

The leader will let each child guess what he feels. As soon as he has guessed that it is an apple, ask him "What color do you think it is?" When he guesses the color, let him pick out the apple from the bag and show it to the group. Should he have guessed that the apple is green, there will be chuckles of laughter if the children find that the apple he pulls from the bag is red or yellow. Let him replace the apple and another child guess the color until all who wish have an opportunity to feel in the bag, guess the color, and show which one they felt.

Then the children may sit on the chairs not arranged in a circle but informally placed close to the leader or they may take their places around the table. Whichever arrangement is decided upon, each child will be given a quarter of a paper napkin. The leaders will pare the apples since some parents do not wish their children to have the skins of fruit. The apples may be cut into thin slices and passed to the children.

The song, "Church," substituting the word "apples" may be sung as a grace or a brief prayer may be offered. "Thank you, God, for apples," or "Thank you, God, for apples, red, yellow, and green," or

"We like apples. Thank you, God, for apples" are suggestions for prayers that may be used. Encourage the use of the words "please" and "thank you" as apples are passed. There should be several thin slices for each child.

After the luncheon of apples, the children will again be encouraged to use their napkins to wipe their mouths and hands and then place the napkins in the wastebasket or paper bag.

Activities enjoyed during previous sessions may be repeated.

Children may wish to play driving to a roadside market. The boxes and boards used for playing supermarket may become the roadside stand. Big blocks, chairs, or a board placed across two chairs may become the car for driving to the market.

As you hand each child the picture card for today, call attention to the picture. "This girl and boy are doing what we did in nursery class today. Be sure to tell Mother all about the fun we had with apples." *My Picture Card*, Number 8, is for use today.

As children leave, use a small safety pin to pin on notes telling parents of any Thanksgiving enterprise in which the children are to participate. Notes should be mailed to absentees.

FOURTH SUNDAY

If Thanksgiving Day precedes this Sunday, use these plans for sharing on the third Sunday.

The box or basket for receiving gifts brought by the children may be in evidence. If there has been no plan for such sharing and the nursery child brings a can or package because an older brother or sister has done so, accept the gift and express appreciation. No special mention of these gifts will be made to the other children. Permit the children to play with the things they bring, talking about how good canned milk, canned peaches, fresh apples, or other foods are and how glad we are that we can share these with our good friends.

In addition to activities enjoyed on other Sundays this month, children will enjoy any book that gives special emphasis to food.

Play having Thanksgiving dinner. Give the children an opportunity to tell if they are going visiting, having guests, or eating downtown. Tell the story, "We Give Thanks," *My Book for Fall*, page 33, whenever you have an opportunity to do so. This may be read and the picture shown to a group at the tea table, near the picture rail, in the book center, and at the block center.

Puzzles may be enjoyed for a quiet activity.

Provide for some jumping about, perhaps with big muscle equipment, or in playing such a game as "Now I'm Very, Very Small," page 207.

When the children are ready to leave, some of them may wish to take home the food they brought.

If there were five Sundays in either October or November, give the children *My Picture Card*, Number 13, this week. This will leave four cards, one for each Sunday in December.

If there were four Sundays in October and November and five Sundays in December, *My Picture Card*, Number 8, will be used on the last Sunday in November and the last five cards will be used, one on each of the five Sundays in December.

December

SO MANY INTERESTING AND LOVELY THINGS COME TO MIND AS YOU plan for December in the nursery class that it is wise to remember the importance of maintaining an atmosphere of peace and good will. Do not crowd the children with too many new and exciting ideas and suggestions. Select a few things to do, remain calm and controlled yourself, and help keep the children happy and calm. If you can arrange to have your room open and some of your workers present for a morning or afternoon several times during the month, you may render a real service to children and their mothers by inviting the children to spend a few hours there. Mother, freed to shop or make preparations at home without the children, will appreciate this service. Children will be happier than they will be if taken into crowds of shoppers.

Purpose

To help the children think of Christmas as the birthday of Jesus; to think of Jesus the Baby who was loved and cared for by his family, as they are loved and cared for by their families; to provide happy times for children.

Suggested Bible Study for Teachers

Read, reread, and memorize the Christmas story from Luke 2:1-20. Read the story from Matthew 1:18 through 2:15. Participate in vesper and other adult worship services during the Christmas season. Take advantage of any opportunities you have to enjoy beautiful music, art, poetry, and prose which will enrich your feeling of wonder and love during this season. Keep Christmas in your own heart and life in order that you may share its spirit with all children with whom you come in contact.

Preparations for December Sessions

Put away books and pictures used during October and November which will not contribute to your purpose during December.

Clip and mount magazine pictures showing Christmas activities of individual children or family groups. You may include other pictures of Jesus as a baby in addition to the one in *Nursery Class Pictures*.

If teachers or other adults in the church are willing to provide new toys or equipment during the season, select them with care. Perhaps a new baby doll, with soft blanket for wrapping, a small rocking chair, some new books, a strong, sturdy truck, or a Madonna picture may be added.

Since children receive so many gifts, share with parents your plans to provide new things for the room for all of the children instead of giving individual gifts.

If the children are to participate in some church-wide giving project emphasize that we share toys or gifts with others because we want them to be happy.

When children talk of Santa Claus, comment, "We can play Santa, too. It is fun to give gifts at Christmas, because it is Jesus' birthday."

Have Christmas greens, berries, cones, and so on for the children to handle, look at, and smell. They may even taste.

Small bells should be provided for the children's enjoyment. Sew or tie two or three bells on a piece of tape to fit the child's wrist. Provide several sets of such bells.

Add to the reading center: *Jesus the Little New Baby* and *Jesus the Children's Friend* by Mary Edna Lloyd.

Secure a few figures and make a simple crèche or manger scene.

Make provision for one or more small Christmas trees and simple unbreakable ornaments, bits of tinsel, and silver icicles.

Secure and sign Christmas greeting cards to mail to each child.
A few gift boxes of assorted sizes will be needed for dramatic
play of delivering gifts.

Provide clay, a small red or green candle, and wax paper. Prepare
a note to go with the candle. Such a note may say,

> DEAR PARENTS,
> You and your nursery class child may watch this
> candle burn as you enjoy the Christmas story found
> in *My Book for Fall*, page 47, or Luke 2:8-12.
> May you have a happy Christmas.

NURSERY CLASS TEACHER

If the nursery class is to give a gift to the sexton, such as a necktie
or handkerchief, this gift should be ready. Wrappings and many seals
will be needed. (See page 120.)

If a card is to be sent to the minister or some other member of
the church staff be sure that it is ready to be "signed" by the children.

Those persons who received the gift or the cards may be invited
to stop in to thank the children at a later session.

If practicable, invite a mother to bring her baby into the group for
a few minutes of one session. Be sure to tell her at what time in the
session it will be best for her to come.

As you plan for each session, remember that three-year-olds may
ignore the exciting new things and continue to enjoy familiar routines.
Avoid strenuous efforts to distract them. They will have many years
in which to do the special things.

Stories to Be Used During December

It is better to have a few books or stories available to be used and
enjoyed in the book center than to have a great number. Each book
should be placed there because it will help teachers to share ideas with
children.

Every teacher should know the stories well enough to tell them
whenever opportunity presents itself. This may be through telling one
story over and over again or it may be through telling several stories.
For some children conversation or a few short sentences while looking
at pictures may be as much of a story as they are ready for.

While a story is suggested for each Sunday, you will find that the children enjoy hearing familiar ones several times. Do not hesitate to tell them more than once. You may be asked to tell several different stories. As you tell the stories from *My Book for Fall*, remind the children that this story is in the book which they have at home. Suggest that they ask someone to read the Christmas stories and sing the songs in *My Book for Fall*.

SUGGESTED PROCEDURE

FIRST SUNDAY

As children arrive, greet them pleasantly, help them to hang wraps and put purses, muffs, gloves, and other possessions on the shelf above the rack.

As they put money into the container, you may wish to comment that our church uses some of its money to help people have happy times at Christmas.

During the session, call each child's attention to pictures of Jesus and his family. If you have several pictures you may say, "This is the way someone thought the Baby and his mother looked."

You may choose to leave that comment for later years, simply calling attention to the loving care given to the Baby by his mother, by Joseph, and by others who came to see him. Emphasize the ways in which Jesus was like all babies who are loved and cared for.

If arrangements have been made for a mother and baby to visit, they should come during this session. The children may see how the mother holds the baby. They will enjoy looking at the baby's feet and hands and watching the facial expressions. Be sure that the children do not get too close to the baby. Speak of the care their mothers gave them when they were babies.

If a story is told, use "The First Christmas," *My Book for Fall*, page 36.

If there are new dolls or other playthings, call attention to them. If they were given to the group, mention that they were given to us. You may offer a prayer of gladness to God that friends love us and give us nice things to enjoy at Christmas. Sing often "What Is Christmas?" page 216.

The small bells may be worn around the wrist or held by the children as they sing as they play with the bells, "Merry Christmas to You," to the tune of "Happy Birthday to You."

Playing with bells may be enjoyed more while the children rock in the rocking boat and a teacher sings to them or as they jump about. Such bells may be given to the children to take home, suggesting that the bells may be used for decorating the Christmas tree at home.

Encourage the children to handle the Christmas greens, cones, and bright berries. Crush those with pungent odors and smell them and talk of how good they look and smell. Break open a berry or cone so that the children may see the seeds inside. Comment that birds and squirrels eat the berries and seeds. That is one way God helps them to have food.

Enjoy the new pictures at the various centers, talking about each of them. Included should be some mounted pictures of children singing Christmas songs, families around Christmas trees, and other experiences three-year-olds may enjoy.

Call attention to the books, *Jesus, the Little New Baby* and *Jesus, the Children's Friend.* You may do no more than look at these on this first Sunday, commenting that one tells stories about Jesus when he was a baby, the other about him when he was a grown man.

As children leave, one or two teachers may request parents to be sure to tell the Christmas stories from *My Book for Fall* and sing carols with their children.

Be sure that each child has a copy of *My Picture Card*, Number 9.

SECOND SUNDAY

Some time preceding Christmas Day, mail to each child a Christmas greeting card. With everyone else in the family receiving mail, this will bring special pleasure to the three-year-old.

Be sure to have the gift for the sexton, wrapping paper, seals, ribbon, and the enclosure card ready if you plan to wrap the gift this Sunday.

As children come, greet them by name and see that each selects his own name tag. As children place their offering in the container provided for it, repeat the comment that our church uses some of its money to help people have happy times at Christmas. Call attention to pictures, books, and other activities. Repeat the play with bells and the Christmas song using them.

Encourage the children to listen to the pianist or to recorded music of Christmas carols. One or several children at a time will enjoy this. Many in the group may enjoy the music while playing at various centers. Do not urge the entire group to do so at one time. Three-year-olds will enjoy handling the figures and hearing about the people and animals in a simple manger scene. Mary, Joseph, the Baby Jesus, a shepherd, and a few animals may all or some of them be included.

While three-year-olds may see pictures and hear about angels who sang at Jesus' birth, it is better to omit the angels in order to avoid suggesting areas of thought about which you are unable to answer questions. You may find it wise to include only the Holy Family and the animals. The figures should be attractive, and, if possible, unbreakable. As children handle the figures, speak of them as dolls made to look like Mary, Joseph, Jesus, and the animals. Some small children have been known to think of the figures as actually being Mary, Joseph, or the Baby.

Sing "Little Baby Jesus," page 215, or "Away in a Manger," page 212. No attempt will be made to teach the carol, "Away in a Manger," but many will have heard it at home and may sing with you.

The small Christmas tree may be enjoyed for several Sundays. A few unbreakable ornaments and some bits of tinsel and silver icicles may be put on and taken off. Use some of the little bells for decorations. Children like to take hold of hands and move around the tree. Sing "What Is Christmas?" page 216, or "Christmas Morning," page 217, or make up a song, such as

> "We like to trim our Christmas tree,
> We like to make it pretty.
> We like to go around and around,
> Around our Christmas tree."

Children may make suggestions which can be made part of the song and play. After the children have enjoyed the play, each group may be ready to sit down around it and listen to a story. Tell "Merry Christmas," *My Book for Fall*, page 41, and encourage discussion about surprises for others.

In the housekeeping center, suggest that children wrap the baby doll and rock him to sleep. Sing about "Little Baby Jesus." In the block center, wooden farm animals may be enjoyed and moved around as the story "Merry Christmas" is told.

When possible it is nice to plan for the nursery class to give the sexton a gift, probably a necktie, handkerchief or something similar. Show the gift to the children. Explain that it is to be a surprise, so we must keep the secret—not tell our sexton. Let the children wrap the package, tie the ribbons and put on the gummed seals. Let them decide where to put the package until the Sunday before Christmas when they will present it.

As the children leave at the close of the session, comment on the happy time you have enjoyed with them, adding, "See you next Sunday." Give each child *My Picture Card,* Number 10.

THIRD SUNDAY

As the children arrive, greet each one personally, help him dispose of his wraps, place his money in the offering container, and find something interesting to do.

The Christmas trees may still be enjoyed.

A few boxes may be added to the Christmas tree play for this session. Suggest that the children play delivering gifts. Continue enjoyment of activities suggested for other Sundays during this month.

If Christmas comes during the week following this session, you may wish to encourage children to prepare a candle to take home. A small red or green candle is placed in a ball of clay, play dough, or wallpaper cleaner so that it will stand up when placed on a table or window sill. When the clay is dry it will become quite hard. The note suggesting that the family may enjoy burning the candle during the telling of the Christmas story, may be tied to the candle. The candles in their holders may be kept at the church until dry or wrapped in wax paper to be carried home today.

Some churches give a large red candle to each child, with the note, and encourage the parents to burn the candle and tell the Christmas story or sing carols each evening. The large candle may be wrapped to carry home. Be sure that the candle and note are carried to each child who is absent.

If a gift has been planned for the sexton it should be delivered to him at this time. The children should have the fun of putting on extra seals.

If the card for the minister and/or other members of the church staff, is to be signed, encourage the children to "write" their names. This may appear to the adult as mere scribbling. Do not guide the child's hand to form his name or expect him to print even an initial. The leader will add the words, "From the Nursery Class," and address the card.

You may wish to tell to small groups of children the story, "The Christmas Story," *My Book for Fall,* page 47. Explain that the stories about Jesus are in the Bible, showing them an attractive copy of the Book.

Show the picture, "When Jesus Was a Baby." Call attention to various items of interest, such as the swaddling cloths.

As children go home, you may tell each of them, "We have happy times together at Christmas time and all through the year." You may wish to sing one of the Christmas songs to each child or small group of children as they leave. Be careful to provide reassurance to those children who are called for late. Give each *My Picture Card*, Number 12, if this is the Sunday before Christmas. Otherwise, give card Number 11. Sing "Merry Christmas" to the tune of "Happy Birthday," as the children leave.

FOURTH SUNDAY

If the fourth Sunday comes after Christmas, children will need quiet activities, such as enjoying picture books and playing with puzzles and clay. They may need opportunities to talk about the gifts they have received. Some may bring new toys or dolls to show. If so, they should be encouraged to show them to other children, then place them on the shelf above their wraps for safekeeping until time for going home. Some three-year-olds are willing to share new toys, others are not. Young children cannot share until they are secure in the feeling of ownership or possession. One cannot share that which he does not truly feel is his own. Those who are not yet ready to share, should not be scolded. The suggestion that the new possession be put away, in plain view for safekeeping, is likely to free the child from concern over its safety while he enjoys his usual activities.

Play, songs, stories, and enjoyment of pictures already familiar may be profitably used again, or tell the story, "After-Christmas Fun," *My Book for Fall*, page 50. It may be that no story will be needed for this Sunday.

If the children have given a simple gift to the sexton, the minister, or some other member of the church staff, that person may come by to tell them of his appreciation for their kindness. They may enjoy singing "Little Baby Jesus" for the guest. Three-year-olds are more likely to listen than to sing.

If December has five Sundays and this is the Sunday before Christmas, tell "The Christmas Story," *My Book for Fall*, page 47, use the picture, "When Jesus Was a Baby," and give each child *My Picture Card*, Number 12.

FIFTH SUNDAY

If there is a fifth Sunday in December, it will follow Christmas. Procedure suggested for last Sunday may be followed.

Leave out for several Sundays some of the things children have enjoyed during Christmas, including the Christmas trees. Adults are sometimes weary of evidences of Christmas, but children would enjoy prolonging its pleasures indefinitely.

On the last Sunday in December, children should be free to enjoy puzzles, block building, or new toys that they may bring from home. Provide opportunities for a picture walk. Two or three children may go with one teacher, stopping on their walk around the room to look at the Christmas pictures. Encourage conversation by the children. If interest warrants, tell the story about one or two of the pictures.

The teacher may speak of the fact that another special day is coming. We call this special day, "New Year's Day." Friends say to one another, "Happy New Year." Sing "Happy New Year to You" to the tune of "Happy Birthday."

Watch for evidences of fatigue. These may be crossness, restlessness, or just a need for sitting quietly and doing nothing. Plan for alternating quiet and active play in order to help children avoid over-excitement and weariness.

As children's parents call for them, express your satisfaction in having been permitted to share their child's pleasure during this blessed season and wish each child and his parents a happy New Year.

If December has five Sundays, October and November probably had four Sundays each. Therefore, *My Picture Card*, Number 13 will be given today.

At the End of the Month

How much have you helped the children to begin to think of Christmas as the birthday of Jesus? In what ways have you renewed your own faith this Christmastide?

WINTER QUARTER

VERY EARLY IN THE QUARTER, COPIES OF *My Book for Winter* should be delivered to the three-year-olds. Secure the books before the first Sunday and fill in each child's name on page 3. Each teacher should sign his or her own name on pages 2 and 3. It is good to give the address and telephone number of the superintendent, or at least one worker, so that the parents may know how to get in touch with the teachers. Each worker should reread "Some Special Problems," pages 22 to 31, as well as the suggested teachers' helps for the entire quarter, pages 124 to 147. It is also important to read all of the material for children and adults in *My Book for Winter*. Each month, each teacher will also read the pages in *Child Guidance in Christian Living* devoted to work with three-year-olds as well as all of the magazine section of that teacher's magazine.

If the teacher has carefully studied suggestions for the entire quarter, it will be quite easy to make necessary adjustments to meet unexpected opportunities. For example, the father-teacher in one nursery class had read all suggestions for the winter quarter. He knew that the snow story did not come on the first Sunday in January. But it snowed that Saturday night. Being a good nursery class teacher, he was ready! He took a sled to church with him. He took a large piece of dark cloth to catch the few lazy snowflakes still falling. There was real sharing and there was real worship in that nursery class that morning. The suggestions for that first Sunday in January were used later in the quarter.

In one part of the country, there was a fresh snowfall three weekends during the winter quarter. Other suggestions for those Sundays were put aside. Snow and God's care for us was the emphasis on snowy Sundays. Nursery teachers in those church schools, alert to the interests of their children, followed those interests, enjoyed snow.

The teacher should always be fully prepared—this means having ready for use much more than will or can be used at any one session, then, following the lead of the children and also guiding them, that well-prepared teacher is ready for *real* teaching.

It is well to help parents at all times to be alert to the child's emotional and physical fitness for group participation. But safeguarding physically is especially necessary during the winter months.

A note to each parent, pinned to the child's wraps, or mailed on a post card, may call attention to the parents' message in *My Book for Winter*, page 2. Or, a special note may be written,

DEAR FATHER AND MOTHER:

At this time of year colds develop rapidly and spread easily. The "common cold" often proves to be the first sympton of measles, whooping cough, chickenpox, and so on. To safeguard the health of each member of the group it is necessary that parents co-operate with the nursery workers by keeping their children at home when they have developed colds or have been exposed to any contagious disease.

This precaution is not only for the other members of the group, but also for the child who has even the slight cold. His resistance is lowered and he is more likely to contract any other illness with which he might come in contact.

Cordially yours,

NURSERY CLASS LEADER

In case a child is ill, or becomes so, during a session his parents should be sent for. If they cannot be reached he should be separated from the other children for his own sake and for the protection of the group. Any toys with which he plays should be thoroughly disinfected.

During the quarter, areas of experience which will be emphasized include: Community Helpers; Friends; Birds; Winter Weather; and Jesus, Friend of Children. You will note that the stories and suggested activities are built around shared family experiences.

Since there are such wide variations in weather in different sections of the country, plans may have to be shifted from one Sunday to another in order that activities may be timely.

In the effort to help children learn to know and appreciate such community helpers as the doctor and postman, one of these should be asked to visit the group. Many groups have had valuable experiences visiting with the doctor. Before issuing the invitation, be sure to reread "Visitors," page 67.

January

POSSIBLE MATERIALS AND ACTIVITIES

Possible Stories for January (select from these stories in *My Book for Winter*, Part 2): "When Friends Come to Play," "Feeding the Birds," "Warm Snowsuits," "My Doctor," "Fun in the Snow."

Possible Songs for January: "The Redbird," "My Friends," "The Snowman," "Church," "Winter Fun."

Possible Pictures for January: "Feeding the Birds," from *Nursery Class Pictures.* See also page 127.

Possible Activities for January: Talk about warm clothing when weather is cold. Enjoy big muscle play. Look at bowls of bulbs. Feed winter birds. Play snowman. Enjoy housekeeping play. Enjoy visit from a doctor. Play doctor and nurse.

My Picture Card: Select from January, February, March.

Purpose

To help children enjoy winter weather as they more fully appreciate warm clothing; to learn more about birds and delight in helping to feed them; to hear about the doctor and his work.

Suggested Bible Study for Teachers

Read several of Paul's letters, especially those to the church at Corinth. Study carefully First Corinthians 12 with its emphasis on the value of a variety of gifts, and chapter 13 of the same letter that describes the true nature of Christian love. Use these two chapters, preferably from the Revised Standard Version, in your meeting as the workers plan together. If possible, attend an adult Bible study group during this quarter. While only a few selected Bible stories and verses are shared directly with three-year-olds, those who teach them should continually read and study the Bible on an adult level.

Preparation for January Sessions

Plan carefully for a variety of activities that permit children opportunity for freedom of choice, use of big muscles, and times of quiet activity.

If a snowy Sunday comes during January, use the snow story, "Fun in the Snow." (See suggestions, page 138.)

Once more, remind yourself that busy, happy children should be let alone, even though you may have prepared interesting things for them to do. Keep in mind that due to differences in age and development, not all of the children will have the same interests or make the same responses to your suggestions. More activities are suggested for each session than any one group is likely to undertake. It is better to be prepared for an activity that is not carried through than to find yourself searching for something with which to entertain or distract restless, disorderly children.

Remove most of the Christmas decorations.

Clip and mount magazine pictures and also those from *My Book for Winter* showing: a doctor; children playing together, feeding birds, wearing warm clothing.

If you plan to have a doctor visit, the purpose of the visit should be carefully explained to him and some guidance given for relating him to the children. For example, ask the doctor to bring his stethoscope. He may also bring a flashlight to look at their throats. You may wish to bring bathroom scales and weigh the children.

Do not expect the children to talk about the visitor a great deal as soon as he is gone. They will likely move back into activities of their own choosing. At home, later, or on another Sunday, they may recall things he said or did and enjoy dramatizing some of his activities as part of their play.

Have ready glass bowls, stones, and narcissus bulbs. Also a picture of narcissus bloom from a florist catalogue.

Add new blankets and some warm clothing for the dolls in the housekeeping area.

A few ramps, fence sections, and short lengths of plank added to the blocks will encourage building of roads and railroad tracks.

A large wheelless, or very sturdy wheeled floor train is a worthwhile investment as it will last for years. Some of the newer ones have Diesel type engines.

Make provisions for feeding the birds at church. Seed for feeding the birds at home may be placed in envelopes and sealed. Children may put a gummed bird seal on each envelope to be taken home.

If there are five Sundays in January, the suggestions for the fifth Sunday in March (page 147) may be adapted. Any story in *My Book for Winter* may be used. A snowy Sunday will provide opportunities to watch the snow falling, to talk about it covering flowers and bulbs and to play "The Snowman," page 208. Such adaptation of plans should always be made when opportunities arise. Likewise in the southern part of our country, first evidences of spring will be used whenever they occur.

Stories to Be Used During January

Each worker should familiarize herself with the contents of the stories so that she may share the idea of each in a few sentences with children who are not ready to hear a full-length story. She may find herself elaborating for children interested in longer stories, or using them as patterns to make up similar narratives about the children in her own group.

Since the children have the entire book to be enjoyed at home and it is not necessary to have a story each Sunday, your use of the books will depend upon the emphasis you choose and the interest of your group of children.

SUGGESTED PROCEDURE

FIRST SUNDAY

As the children arrive, help with their wraps and offering. If the weather is cold, you may comment on how glad we are for nice warm clothing and for a warm church building. You may mention that some of the money we give to the church is used for heat and light. If children wish to talk about Christmas, listen with interest to the things they tell you. Remind them again that Christmas is Jesus' birthday and call attention to the picture of him as a baby with his family. Tell the children again that Mary loved Jesus and took care of him as their mothers loved and cared for them when they were babies.

Encourage children to find interesting things to do.

Clear glass bowls, stones, and narcissus bulbs may be placed on a table. Suggest that the children feel the bulbs. Show a picture of the flower that blooms when they are planted and tell how the bowl is kept in a dark place for a while, then brought out into the light to grow. It is well to provide for several bowls to be planted in case several groups of children are interested. A clear glass bowl permits the children to watch the roots as well as the tops of the plants when they begin to grow. You may wish to include in your prayer that we are glad that we can plant and tend flowers. Recall the bulbs that were planted outdoors last fall.

In the housekeeping center, encourage children to tell what they do at home to help. Since some of them will make unreasonable claims, be prepared to comment that it is fun to play that you prepare the whole meal, make a cake, or wash all the dishes. A table cloth, or some place mats, or a new tea set may make mealtime play more pleasant.

If you have some new doll blankets or warm clothing for the dolls, comment that we all need warm covers and warm clothing when the weather is cold and that we are glad to have mother and father think about getting these things for us.

The children will enjoy looking at and talking about mounted pictures or picture books showing children playing together.

Encourage conversation about sharing new Christmas toys and putting away toys at home and in nursery class. Talk also about the fun of taking turns when they help to set the table (or any other small responsibility that may be delegated to a three-year-old). This conversation may be carried on at the various interest centers as opportunities arise.

Be prepared to tell the story, "When Friends Come to Play," *My Book for Winter*, page 5, at any time and sing "My Friends," page 219.

Big muscle play should be encouraged in order to prevent children from becoming tired of staying indoors. If weather permits and children seem to need the change, let two or three of them at a time put on wraps and with a helper to take a short run up and down the walk outside.

As children go home, mention that we have had a happy time together this first Sunday of the New Year. Again wish each of them a happy New Year and give each *My Picture Card*, Number 1.

SECOND SUNDAY

As the children arrive, greet them, help them hang their wraps and put their money in the container as before. Remind them that some of their money is used to help keep the church warm and clean. Sing "Church," page 224. If there is snow, sing "Winter Fun," page 213.

Help each child to find something interesting to do. Some may be interested in putting water on the bulbs planted in the glass bowls last Sunday. Look at the bowls of bulbs, talking about the white roots going down among the rocks and the green shoots reaching up. Look at the picture of the flower you hope will bloom, and use a prayer similar to: "Dear God, thank you for beautiful flowers. We are glad that we can help them grow."

If snow is on the ground, clear a small area so that the children may feed the birds. Grain, crackers or bread crumbs may be used as feed. Be sure the crumbs provided are clean and fresh enough for nibbling, as some of the children will surely taste the food. Comment that birds eat seeds and berries, but that in cold weather they need our help. Offer a prayer, "We are glad that we can help the birds find something to eat. Thank you, God, for birds." Have pictures of birds and a bird book for the children to look at.

Sing "The Redbird," page 218, and show large picture, "Feeding the Birds."

Tell the story, "Feeding the Birds," *My Book for Winter*, page 9, to one or a few children at a time if there are opportunities.

Small groups may play "The Snowman," page 208.

In the housekeeping center, suggest the play of preparing a meal, baking a cake, and washing the dishes.

Some children may wish to draw at the easel or on the floor. Encourage big muscle play through building with big blocks, rocking in the boat, turning the boat over, and jumping from it to the floor.

When the children leave, make a comment to each one about something you have observed that he enjoyed. Call attention to the picture on *My Picture Card*, Number 2, that each child is to take home today.

THIRD SUNDAY

As the children arrive, teachers will encourage self help in removing and hanging wraps. While doing so, speak of their sweaters, coats, ski suits, and so on. Speak of the warm wraps and of the mothers and daddies who care for the boys and girls and keep them warm when they go outdoors. It is quite likely that the children will mention their rubbers or galoshes that they wear in the snow and that new gloves will be exhibited for approval. This is in preparation for later telling of the story, "Warm Snowsuits," *My Book for Winter*, page 12.

Feeding the birds and talking about them should be enjoyed for many Sundays. If birds come to the feeding space, children will enjoy watching them.

In the housekeeping center, repeat your play of preparing and serving, eating, and cleaning up after meals. This play will provide opportunities for the prayer, "Thank you, God, for our food."

Some children may again enjoy drawing.

Keep in mind that all of these suggestions are not likely to be followed by any one group of workers and children. It is not necessary that each child hear a story. Stories are told when children seem interested and are ready for them.

As each child leaves, recall something that he has enjoyed. Perhaps you will comment on his new galoshes, gloves, or his warm coat.

Give each one *My Picture Card*, Number 3.

FOURTH SUNDAY

As children arrive, greet them individually, help them with wraps, and call attention to the receptacle for the offering. You may wish to ask who gave them the money, and express gladness for parents, grandparents, or others who give us money to bring to church.

Since several suggestions for activity have been offered this month, you may feel it unwise to launch any new enterprise during this session. If so, continue to enjoy activities already familiar, including play at the various interest centers. Perhaps some of the children have been absorbed in one of the suggested activities and have not yet participated in others. You may wish to help them to discover the activities enjoyed by others on previous Sundays.

If you feel that your group is ready to move to a new interest, you may begin to call their attention to some of the numerous people in the community who work to make life safe, happy, and comfortable for many others. These may be introduced over a period of several months. They will include the doctor, the postman, and the policeman.

While the children may continue to play preparing meals, building with blocks, and so on, and may feed the birds throughout the cold months, your group is probably ready now to think of one community helper. The doctor is suggested. You will wish to have the pictures showing a doctor ready to show to the children. Encourage conversation about the pictures.

If you have invited the doctor to come for a visit to your group, it would be well to have ready the story and picture of this helper. Be sure that you talk over with the person invited to come, the things you hope he will do and say, and the way you hope the children will feel about him after his visit. He should come after the children have arrived and are busy.

Take the doctor from group to group, introducing him to the children and telling them something of what he does to make life good for the people of the community. Move away and permit him to talk to the children. Suggest that he show the children his stethoscope and talk of using it to listen to their chests. You will probably offer a prayer of thanks for the good doctors who help us to keep well and to get well when we are sick.

Previous experiences with doctors may have aroused fears or antagonism in a child. If so, do not force this child to approach the doctor. Let him watch from a distance. It may be that another child can carry the stethoscope to the fearful one and so help him establish a new relationship with the doctor.

Such comments may be heard as, "Doctors hurt." "Nurses give shots. They hurt." You may reply truthfully, "Yes, our friend the doctor (or nurse) does sometimes give us shots or bad-tasting medicine. He does it to help us get well or keep well. He is our good friend. We will try to help him when we are hurt or must take unpleasant medicine."

The suggestions in *My Book for Winter* should guide adults at home to help children develop good attitudes toward the doctor friend. The helpful things done by the doctor should be called to mind with emphasis on his care for children.

You may be able to provide an old purse or handbag that resembles the bag carried by the doctor. Put in this some empty plastic bottles and suggest that children in the housekeeping area play that the doll is sick. Mention things the nurse, the mother, the doctor, and the others do to help a sick child feel better. There may be no interest in such play on this Sunday, but it may come later.

If a story is used, tell "My Doctor," *My Book for Winter*, page 16.

Sing the song, "My Friends," page 219, mentioning the doctor or sing "Church," page 224, substituting the word "doctor."

Give each child who wishes to do so, a chance to tell you who his doctor is, commenting that the doctor suggests ways in which we may keep well and grow larger and stronger. If you brought the bathroom scales, weigh the children.

As the children go home, tell each a personal good-by and give him *My Picture Card*, Number 4.

February

POSSIBLE MATERIALS AND ACTIVITIES

Possible Stories for February (select from these stories in *My Book for Winter*, Part 2): "Baby Sister," "Jesus and the Children," "The Postman," "Fun in the Snow."

Possible Songs for February: "Friends at Church," "My Friends," "Church."

Possible Pictures for February: "Jesus and the Children," "When Jesus Was a Baby," and "Baby Sister," from *Nursery Class Pictures.* See also, page 134.

Possible Activities for February: Entertain a postman. Repeat play of doctor and nurse. Enjoy a mother and baby visitor. Make simple valentines and play delivering mail. Feed the birds. Enjoy snow play.

My Picture Card: Select from January, February, March.

IT IS SUGGESTED THAT DURING FEBRUARY, TEACHERS IN THE NURSERY class shall work together to help three-year-olds think of Jesus, the loving friend of children. If appreciation for the doctor was emphasized last month it may be continued. The postman will be introduced as part of the enjoyment of Valentine's Day.

Since February is likely to bring snow, ice, and extremely cold weather to some, and windy days to others, the children may be led to appreciate the beauty, value, and interesting phases of winter weather. It is important that childen recognize the many persons who provide us with protection and comfort against the disagreeable aspects of winter weather. It is also important to help children to make the best of good weather and bad.

Purpose

To provide opportunity for the children to hear another story about Jesus and to learn how they may help care for younger brothers and sisters; to help them enjoy the beauty and fun of wintertime; to appreciate the work of the postman.

Suggested Bible Study for Teachers

The beauty of Psalms 147 as it describes winter weather makes it worthy of many readings. Its poetry is the type that is best appreciated when shared through reading aloud. Perhaps you will decide to memorize it. This, like other suggested biblical materials, is for your enjoyment and enrichment, not for sharing with three-year-olds.

Read and study the story of Jesus and the children in Matthew 19:13-15; in Mark 10:13-16; and in Luke 18:15-17.

You will find it profitable to study the life of Christ. You may like a guide to a better understanding of the Gospels. Perhaps your minister has a book to lend you.

Preparation for February Sessions

Since winter weather is likely to keep you indoors, plan to have some growing things in the room, such as bulb flowers in bloom or green house plants.

Prepare to feed the birds and to call children's attention to beautiful and interesting things to be seen as they look out the window.

Have ready the picture, "Jesus and the Children." Be sure that it is placed where the children may touch it and low enough to be within the eye range of the three-year-old. You may also wish to place in the Bible, opposite the story, the smaller picture of "Jesus and the Children," found on *My Picture Card.*

Provide pictures of and books about the postman and of people enjoying outdoor fun in winter.

Check creative art supplies and make plans for using them.

Check and perhaps add to puzzles and other puzzle-type toys that provide quiet, interesting occupation for individual children. Choose subjects which will be worth talking about. You may be able to secure puzzles showing a doctor, a nurse, a milkman, a policeman, or a postman. Other puzzle-type toys provide cubes, cones, and blocks of various other shapes to fit into slots. Secure a piece of black material and magnifying glass to examine snowflakes.

Provide material needed for playing the role of doctor and postman.

Check blocks and other building supplies. Farm animals and Wedgie[1] people may be enjoyed at the block center.

Provide for indoor big muscle activity.

If you plan to have a postman visit, invite him and tell him at what time to come and carefully explain that the purpose of his visit is to help nursery class children appreciate the friend who brings

---

[1] Wedgie Wood Play People or Stationary or Bendable Rubber Play People available from nursery and kindergarten supply houses. See *Child Guidance in Christian Living* for further information.

mail—especially valentines. Ask the postman to bring his mail bag.

Have ready small lace paper doilies and small gummed hearts or other valentine seals and envelopes. Also a large paper bag with empty envelopes to play postman.

If the mother with her baby who visited at Christmas time is to be invited for the second Sunday, be sure to issue the invitation early in the week.

SUGGESTED PROCEDURE

FIRST SUNDAY

Greet the children, helping them with wraps, and suggesting that they put their money for the church into the container provided for it. Help each child to find something interesting to do. Adults may tire of always having the same activities. But three-year-olds welcome the familiar. It is likely that they will spend a few minutes with one activity and then change to another.

If the postman was invited, take him from group to group, introducing him to the children. Explain that he always wears a gray suit and hat when he brings our mail. He always carries over his shoulder a big bag for letters. Suggest that he show the bag. Guide conversation toward valentines.

Offer a prayer of thanks for the postman friend.

As the children look at the picture of the postman, you may wish to tell the story, "The Postman," *My Book for Winter,* page 25. Sing the song, "My Friends," page 219, using the word, "postman."

Children at the housekeeping center may wish to repeat the play of doctor and nurse for sick dolls. There may also be interest in playing postman. You may thank God, in a simple prayer, for good doctors and nurses who help us to get well when we are sick and for friendly postmen who bring us letters.

Be alert to provide enough active play and enough quiet play to provide interest for children without overtiring. Keep in mind that if children are busy and happy, you do not need to interrupt to talk to them about helpers. They will hear of them often when they are in the kindergarten group.

As children leave, you may comment to them that you have enjoyed thinking with them about our many friends.

Give each child *My Picture Card,* Number 5.

SECOND SUNDAY

As children arrive, greet them, suggesting that they help themselves as much as possible with wraps. If weather is very bad and leggings or snowsuits are worn, you may have to appeal to mothers to help remove these because of the time it takes, especially if most of the children come in at about the same time. If children's garments are not marked with their names, you may suggest that this must be done to prevent mixups.

As money is placed in the offering container, you may comment that money is used to keep our church warm and clean and that we are glad we can each help to do this.

If the mother and baby were invited for today, they may be seated at one side of the room. The children may go singly or in groups of two or three to see the baby. They may talk about the way the baby has grown. The mother will mention ways in which she takes care of the baby and if there is an older brother or sister, the mother will tell of ways older children help, also. Encourage conversation as to ways they help care for a baby brother or sister.

Call attention of small groups of children to the picture of mother and little girl helping to care for the baby. Talk together about ways in which the children help care for the baby at home. Tell the story, "Baby Sister," *My Book for Winter,* page 21, and show the picture.

A few lace paper doilies, heart or other valentine seals, and envelopes will be used for making valentines.

A mail bag may be used with empty envelopes for any child who wishes to play postman. The mail bag is made by tying a band of cloth to a heavy paper bag. Provide several mail bags so that any child who wishes to do so may "deliver mail."

Teachers may wish to mail valentines to the children at their home address. A government postcard, a valentine seal, and a happy Valentine greeting will probably be more attractive and more appropriate than those you might purchase.

If you have a set of Wedgie people, perhaps some of them will be dressed to look like the doctor, the nurse, and the postman. These will be used in block play, conversation, and simple dramatization.

Keep in mind that these suggestions may not prove interesting to all or even a few three-year-olds. Do not coerce those who prefer to follow their own pursuits. Keep your teaching on an individual or small-group basis. Each teacher should be alert to offer a suggestion to any child who seems in need of guidance. Such ongoing activities as use of big muscle equipment, enjoyment of the music or reading centers, looking out the window to see if the birds are eating from the feeding space, and amusing themselves with floor toys and blocks, may occupy all of the time and attention of most of the children.

If the bulbs planted some weeks ago have bloomed, call attention to them. Smell them, talk of the way in which we have enjoyed them. One or two children may go with an adult to take a bowl of blooming bulbs to be placed on a table where they may be enjoyed by those attending the morning worship service. This will, of course, be done on whatever Sunday the flowers are in bloom.

If children suggest activities, respond to their suggestions. Do not dominate the children or their play. Children learn by doing. Workers should be resource persons, not directors of activities.

"Friends at Church," page 214, may be sung as the children put on their wraps. As the children leave the room, give each one the valentine he made in addition to *My Picture Card*, Number 6. Remind him to tell Mother and Daddy about the baby on the card.

THIRD SUNDAY

As children arrive, greet them, help them with wraps and offering. Listen to and comment on the things they have to tell you. Be sure that your attention is given to the children instead of to other adults.

Have a picture of "Jesus and the Children" near the offering container. You may wish to have the Bible nearby, too. Call each child's attention to the picture, commenting that this is a picture of Jesus with some children who were his friends.

Call attention to the book, *Jesus, the Little New Baby*.[1] You may say, "We have enjoyed the book about Jesus when he was a little new baby. Last Sunday a baby and his mother came to visit us." Encourage recall and conversation about care of little babies. "When Jesus was a baby, his mother cared for him. (Show picture, "When Jesus Was a Baby.") He grew and grew, just as you grew from a baby to a bigger boy. Then he grew to be a man."

Show the book, *Jesus the Children's Friend*.[1] "Now we will enjoy this book about Jesus when he grew up to be a man who loved children." You may wish to comment that the person who wrote these books found the stories in the Bible. Show the children the Bible.

---

[1] By Mary Edna Lloyd. May be secured from The Methodist Publishing House serving your territory.

Follow the procedures in interest centers and play as on other Sundays. Encourage small groups of two or three children to sing around the piano.

Show the picture, "Jesus and the Children."

Tell the story, "Jesus and the Children," from *My Book for Winter*, page 28, to any child or children who are interested. Or, look at *Jesus, the Children's Friend* and tell a running story, not necessarily trying to read the words as in the book. If each teacher is alert for opportunities to do so, either of these stories may be shared with each child a number of times during the year. It is suggested for this particular Sunday to provide opportunity for suggesting ways in which such a story may be used. It should not be limited to use during this time only.

After the story and the picture have been enjoyed, pray, "Dear God, we are glad for Jesus the friend of children. Amen."

Some may be interested in playing postman again this Sunday. There may be an interest in telling about valentines received.

As children leave, give them their picture of Jesus and the children as it appears on *My Picture Card*, Number 7.

FOURTH SUNDAY

As children arrive greet them, comment on how good it is to have nice warm clothes if the weather is cold. As they put their offering into the container, sing, "Church," page 224.

The procedures suggested for this Sunday will be used if and when you have snowy weather. It should not be used unless you actually have snow, therefore it is impossible to put it into the materials on a definite time schedule. If there is no snowy weather in your part of the country, the teacher will decide whether it would be wise to attempt to create an interest in snow. One teacher who lives in a semi-tropical part of our country says, "We take a flower walk on the Sundays the lesson material suggests that we think about snow. We look for all the beautiful flowers in bloom at that season." She added, "We had a professional photographer make colored movies of our children playing in snow on the only snowy Sunday I can recall."

Another teacher, in a southern climate, reports, "Of course, we include snow stories and play. It would be too bad to deny the children the fun of snow. Only a few will really have experienced snow play. They cannot imagine how snowflakes look, but we play that we build a snowman and make snowballs."

"The Snowman," page 217, may be enjoyed by all but will be meaningful only to those children who have enjoyed snow play.

Since many more suggestions have been offered for this month than any group is likely to wish to use, you will have no difficulty in planning for a happy session based on activities enjoyed during previous weeks if thinking of snow is inopportune.

On a very snowy Sunday, you may have few children present. This may be the occasion when you can plan to try painting or some other materials not usable with larger numbers of children. Consult pages 80 to 82 of this textbook for suggested procedure. Keep in mind that the value of the experience for three-year-olds is painting, not the production of pictures. They are not likely to paint anything. But, their delight in being privileged to try painting will justify your effort. Short lengths of colored chalk may be dipped into a little water and used to make very pretty "painting."

The children will enjoy looking out the window and talking about the beauty of familiar things when covered with snow. If there are icicles, call attention to them. If an icicle can be broken off and brought inside, the children will enjoy handling it and talking about it. A piece of black velvet or other material can be placed outside the window to catch a few flakes of falling snow. Look at them through the magnifying glass and speak of their beautiful shapes.

Give the children an opportunity to talk of the things they have enjoyed doing at home in the snow. Tell the story, "Fun in the Snow," *My Book for Winter,* page 33, and sing "Winter Fun" page 213.

Sing "Church," page 224, substituting the word "snow."

Comment on the comforts of good warm homes, warm clothing, and hot food in cold weather. Thank God for the pretty snow, for fun in the snow and for warm homes.

As children leave, comment on their enjoyment of snow. Sing the song about snow to each of them.

Give each a copy of *My Picture Card,* Number 8.

March

POSSIBLE MATERIALS AND ACTIVITIES

Possible Stories for March (select from the stories in *My Book for Winter*, Part 2): "Blow, Wind, Blow," "I Like the Dark," "Finger Fun," "Finding a Surprise," "Good Milk to Drink."

Possible Songs for March: "New Chicks," "Friends at Church," "Taking Turns."

Possible Pictures for March: "Feeding the Birds," from *Nursery Class Pictures.* See also, page 141.

Possible Activities for March: Look out the window to watch for objects being moved by the wind. Feed the birds. Play outside in the wind with balloons or kites. Play a simple game. Look for signs of early spring. Plant an outdoor garden or a window box. Listen to music.

My Picture Card: Select from January, February, March.

EASTER WILL SOMETIMES COME DURING MARCH. WHEN AN EARLY Easter date occurs, refer to plans for Easter in the spring quarter, both in the teacher's text and in *My Book for Spring.* The plans suggested for use when the story, "Finger Fun," is to be told may be used at any time throughout the year, and can be omitted to make use of Easter suggestions. Plans for the first Sunday include wind experiences. The suggestions may be used on any windy Sunday.

Whenever children's interest justifies continuing activities built around some attractive theme, you may omit other suggestions. These may be enjoyed at home since the stories for children and suggestions for parents in each copy of *My Book* will introduce the same ideas as those presented in this teacher's textbook. Necessarily, the suggestions for parents are much more limited than those for teachers. You may find that some parents are interested in reading the teacher's textbook, and the suggestions for teachers that appear each month in *Child Guidance in Christian Living.*

Purpose

To help children to enjoy windy weather and to learn how to accept cheerfully the disagreeable phases of it; to provide opportunities to wonder at early spring surprises and planting experiences; to help them enjoy the dark.

Suggested Bible Study for Teachers

You may enjoy taking a concordance and searching through the Bible for references to the wind, the rain, to birds, and flowers. It will prove interesting to you as you think of how closely the Bible is related to man's feeling about God as he observes the evidences of God's handiwork revealed through nature. Read about the wind in Psalms 147:18; of the time of the singing birds in Song of Solomon 2:12. Then turn to the Psalms, and noting descriptions of content at the head of each column, read several songs of praise, as Psalms 92, 95 through 107, Psalms 111 through 113, Psalms 117, 118, 146 through 150.

Cultivate the attitude of thankfulness for beauty, stirring life, and evidences of the loving generosity of the Creator during this month as you help boys and girls rejoice in the happy aspects of blustery windy days and learn to accept pleasantly the less attractive aspects of wind. As you rejoice in the return of spring, you should feel quickening within your own spirit a sense of worship and pleasure in the world in which you live. Religion is communicable. A joyous spirit is contagious. Seek both through a more intimate knowledge of the Bible as the sourcebook of praise.

Preparations for March Sessions

Remove pictures, books, and other items related to last month's emphasis.

Mount and have ready for use pictures showing children flying kites, clothes drying, and trees moving in the wind. Early spring flowers, families planting gardens, children getting ready for bed and sleeping. Have picture, "Feeding the Birds," available for use at any time.

Secure or make picture books about the wind, springtime, and gardening.

If early spring flowers have not yet begun to bloom outdoors in your area, provide some green plants and some branches of pussy willow and forsythia and twigs of tiny leaf buds. Place these on a low table.

Look over supplies and replenish any that are needed.

Check toys, repairing any which are broken and discarding those beyond repair.

Clean all toys and wash doll clothing and bedding. Examine the books. Mend any torn pages.

Provide a clothesline with small clothespins, stretching it near the housekeeping area.

Have balloons ready for each child and a ball of heavy string to tie a length to each of the balloons. Leave a loop at the end of the string to slip over the child's hand. Or, you may prefer to use a kite cut from construction paper, with string attached.

If possible, secure a spot outdoors where your children may dig and plant. If your church has a grounds committee that supervises care of the grounds, it will be necessary to clear permission for a small plot of ground. Eighteen by thirty-six inches will be ample space. Have the sexton spade up the soil in advance of the time you will need it. If there is no garden space available, a window box may be used. (In northern parts of the country these seed-planting plans will be held until the appropriate time—possibly not used until late April.)

Have trowels, small rakes, seeds, and two or three watering cans. Marigolds, zinnias, and nasturtiums are satisfactory flowers as they blossom quickly.

If you wish children to take seeds home, have ready small envelopes containing a few seeds. A simple note may be written on the outside of the envelope, asking that the child be permitted to plant the seeds at home.

Provide flower seals to be pasted on the envelopes.

Check your calendar to find when Easter comes this year. If it comes in March, turn to the plans for the spring quarter and read the suggestions for Easter.

At any time that a crocus blooms on the church lawn or in the garden plot, be sure to use it to help the children sense wonder and the love of a Creator who "causeth the grass (and flowers) to grow."

SUGGESTED PROCEDURE

FIRST SUNDAY

Since the suggestions for this Sunday are for a windy day, you may need to use them on some other Sunday, substituting for this session the plans outlined for that day.

As the children arrive, be at the door to greet them. If the wind is blowing comment on the rosiness of their cheeks. Help with wraps as needed. Guide each child in finding something to do at the interest centers.

Call attention to pictures and picture books. Comment on things the wind does—dries clothes hanging on the line, tosses the trees about, blows hats off, keeps kites moving in the air, and blows papers along the street. If there are pictures of these, some of the children may enjoy looking at them. Others might look out the window to watch for objects being moved by the wind. If you can see people from your window, note the way they walk when the wind is blowing. Try to develop the idea that we cannot *see* the wind, but that we can *feel* it.

The children in the housekeeping center will notice the clothesline and clothespins. Pinning (dry) clothes on the line will be a mechanical operation for the three-year-old. You may mention that God plans for the wind to blow. It dries the clothes more quickly. Mention the sunshine also.

You may have an opportunity to say, "It is such fun to play in the wind. Thank you, God, for happy times playing in the wind. Amen."

The story, "Blow, Wind, Blow," *My Book for Winter,* page 36, may be told.

Suggest that dolls be wrapped in blankets to protect them from the wind and taken for a ride around the room in the doll carriage, wagon, or truck. During the ride around the room, stop to look at the pictures or look out the window to see if there are birds eating at the feeding space.

Note and comment on growing plants and blooming flowers and budding twigs. There may be an opportunity for a brief prayer of thanks to God for springtime beauty.

The older children may draw or paint with damp colored chalk. Comment on the bright colors of the pictures.

Encourage play with puzzles and floor toys as before.

A few children at a time may be taken outside to feel and hear the wind blowing. When you return, comment on the warmth and comfort of our classroom.

Instead of a few children going outside at one time, you may be able to take all of the children who wish to go outside to play in the wind. Enjoyment of this will be increased if they take with them the balloons or kites you have provided. Speak of the way the wind pulls and tugs at the balloons or kites. If an outdoor trip is impossible, you may enjoy a running conversation type of story.

The leader may speak about the wind blowing at night. Some of the children may tell of hearing the wind through the trees and whistling around the house. The snug comfort of bed may be emphasized. "The wind blew and blew but Bobby snuggled down in bed, and Mary snuggled down in bed, and Ruth snuggled down in bed, and Tommy snuggled down in bed. They closed their eyes. The wind whistled and whistled and whistled but all the children went to sleep. They slept until the next morning when it was time to come to nursery class." Names of children in the group may be substituted in the story. The leader may suggest that they go near the window or keyhole or open the door, then they may listen to hear the whistle of the wind. They may softly make the sound that the wind made while they were asleep last night and as it whistles around the church today—"*Whoo-oo-ooo, Whoo-oo-ooo.*"

Give each child *My Picture Card*, Number 9, and a balloon or a kite to take home. Be sure to warn them to hold tightly to the string so that the wind will not play a joke and carry the balloon or kite away.

SECOND SUNDAY

As the children arrive, greet them and help them with wraps if it is necessary. Be interested to listen to what they have to tell you. Many of the children will now know what they want to do as soon as they arrive. Others may need a little encouragement or guidance.

Show the pictures of children asleep and children ready for bed.

Tell the story, "I Like the Dark," *My Book for Winter,* page 41.

Encourage conversation about going to sleep without any light, or watching the moon after they are in bed, or looking out the window with Mother or Daddy to watch the bright lights twinkle on the streets, or seeing the automobiles flash their lights, or just seeing the dark outdoors. Children who have such happy experiences have an undergirding of security that the leader wishes the other members of the group to develop.

"Thank you, God, for nighttime when girls and boys may rest" or "We are glad that we can sleep at night. Thank you, God, for the nighttime and the quiet" may be prayers for this session.

Suggest to the children in the housekeeping area that they put the dolls to bed. They may wish to have them say prayers, or hear a bedtime story. If you have a teddy bear or other soft animal, you may play a game of hunting for it with eyes shut. Three-year-olds do not like to be blindfolded and will not keep their eyes shut, but they will enjoy playing hunting for the toy just the same.

If there is a supply room or closet without a window, the children may take turns peeping into the room or closet to see how dark it is. Make a game of seeing objects in the dark closet. But be very sure that no child goes into the room where it is dark. Have the light turned on if the child steps inside to verify what he saw, as for example, a broom, a mop, or ladder, and so on. The door will never be closed when the children are in the supply room or closet.

There may be a request from the children to go outdoors again to play in the wind. If so, small groups may be taken out to play.

Small groups of children, indoors or out, may enjoy a simple game, such as "Ring Rosy," page 207, or "Teeter-Totter," pages 208 and 220.

As the children go home, comment on the fun we have enjoyed with our friends and give each *My Picture Card,* Number 10.

THIRD SUNDAY

As the children arrive, mention (if it is true in your area) that the grass is growing green, and the flowers are blooming in gay colors.

Call attention to the flowering forsythia or other blooming flowers in the room. Let the children smell and touch them. Say, "Thank you, God, for flowers."

Call attention to pictures and books about digging and planting. If spring has come and you are able to have an outdoor planting experience, the children may go in small groups to the designated place prepared by the sexton. The children will enjoy digging with the trowels, raking the earth, and pushing down the seed. Talk about the picture of the flower on the outside of the seed package. (In many parts of our country this activity will be reserved for at least a month.) Enjoy picture on the card for this session (Number 11).

While planting the seeds, conversation will point to God's part in the ongoing life. "We cannot make the seeds grow. We can help God by planting the seeds, but the rain must come and the sun must shine. Then the flower grows. God makes the flowers to bloom. We can only help as we plant them." This session should hold many opportunities for brief "seconds of worship."

If it is too early to plant seeds, you may wish to tell the story, "Good Milk to Drink," *My Book for Winter,* page 52. There may be housekeeping play of enjoying meals, buying milk from the milkman or from the grocery store or market, serving milk to drink, to use on cereal, or on pudding. Such activity should provide opportunity for a brief thank-you prayer.

If you planted seeds today, plan to give seeds for home planting. Otherwise, this suggestion may be carried out later in the season.

Some may wish to hear the story, "Finding a Surprise," *My Book for Winter*, page 44. If there happens to be a blooming crocus clump on the church lawn, or in a nearby yard, be sure to arrange to go outdoors to see, talk about, and give thanks for this evidence of spring.

If the bulbs planted last fall are through the ground or blooming, plan to take the children outside to see and talk about this. Use opportunities for discussion and for prayer.

As the children go home, give each one his envelope with seeds to plant at home, and *My Picture Card*, Number 11.

FOURTH SUNDAY

As the children arrive, greet them as usual and help each one to find something to do.

Call attention to the pictures of families planting together. Encourage children to tell of happy times their families have. Ask the children if they planted the seeds taken home. Encourage them to talk about it. Some children may be interested in watering the flower garden or window box.

The rocking boat or a plane built of large blocks may be used for playing airplane.

In the housekeeping area, doll play will be encouraged as well as the enjoyment of pinning clothes on the line.

If it is a windy day, enjoy going outdoors again to have fun in the wind.

Provide puzzles and individual toys for those who wish to play alone. Keep in mind that children may not respond to your suggestions and make no effort to force them. Continued enjoyment of familiar activities may have greater value. Enjoy and share these as well as the responses of children who are ready for new ideas and suggestions. Some may wish to listen to the record player.

The children may enjoy hearing the story, "Finger Fun," *My Book for Winter*, page 48. They will find pleasure in moving their fingers as Dianne did. Lack of muscular control makes it difficult for young children to use complicated finger plays, but this simple play will be enjoyed by them. They may request the story on following Sundays for the pleasure of playing with their hands as Dianne did.

Conversation may be guided into the ways hands may be helpful. The children may suggest that they put away toys with their hands and they arrange flowers with their hands.

Further sensory experiences may be included as the feel of green grass and of sand and perhaps the feel of water. Some of the children may tell about going barefooted and feeling the grass or sand or water with their feet.

"Ring Rosy", page 207, or "Getting Ready for Nursery Class," page 208, may be played.

As the children leave, give each *My Picture Card*, Number 12.

FIFTH SUNDAY

If there is a fifth Sunday greet the children as usual.

Enjoy repeating any of the activities, stories, and songs used earlier in the month. Be sure to water the flowers and watch for signs of growth. (If used on fifth Sunday in January, adapt plans.)

Whenever it seems opportune, show the picture and retell the story of "Jesus and the Children," *My Book for Winter*, page 28.

There may be continued interest in the care of the garden or flower box. Doll play and block building may be encouraged.

The children may find great satisfaction in just listening to the music. The pianist may play any of the familiar songs and the children listen as they play around the room in the various interest centers. Or some children may go over to the piano to listen to the music or perhaps to sing with the teacher.

Watch for opportunities in the various interest centers for brief "seconds of worship." These may come as a child rocks a doll or puts her to bed, when looking at flowers in the room, or discovering some evidence of spring while outdoors or looking out the window."

The children may again enjoy playing "Ring Rosy," page 207.

As the children leave, comment on the happy time you have had together. Give each child *My Picture Card*, Number 13, and remind each one to show it to father and mother.

Easter With Three-year-olds

OBSERVANCE OF EASTER IN THE CLASS FOR THREE-YEAR-OLDS should be marked with joy as teachers and children share the beauty of the spring season. The story of the Crucifixion and Resurrection will not be told as children of this age are not mature enough to have this experience. This part of the Easter story is reserved until the child is older. For the three-year-old, Easter is a time for remembering Jesus and rejoicing in the renewing of life around us.

Emphasis in the nursery class will be on beauty all about us at this season. This will include calling attention to blue skies with soft white clouds, birds, green grass, fresh young leaves, the budding and open- ing of lovely spring flowers. Over and over we may share with children our joy and wonder at the unfolding miracle of spring. It is unlikely that the three-year-old will recall last spring. This is the first time that spring awakenings have happened so far as he is aware. You are highly privileged to have a part in this. Your joy and wonder should be shared with him in periods of silence, as well as in words, through actual experiences, pictures, songs, stories, and activi- ties. A teacher's major preparations will be personal worship and rejoicing over the promise of immortal life which is the heart of the Easter message.

You may wish to have a meeting with nursery parents, or share in one with teachers and parents of the entire children's division. Topics of interest for such meetings will include: "What About the Easter Bunny?" "How Shall I Tell My Child About Death?" and "Easter Worship in the Home and Church." Leaflets to use as back- ground for such discussions and distribution to parents may be ordered from Service Department, Box 871, Nashville 2, Tennessee. You will find them listed in the free booklet, *Resources for Workers With Children*. Secure this by writing to the office of your conference board of education or to The Methodist Publishing House serving you. Articles from *Child Guidance in Christian Living* and *The Christian Home* will also be useful in such meetings.

Some workers believe that colored eggs and hunts for them have no place in the church school. Others have accepted the brightly colored eggs as a natural part of the season and plan each year for

148

a party with mothers and children. Usually this party is on Saturday afternoon before Easter.

Brightly colored eggs are hidden, found, rehidden, and refound. Refreshments add to the fellowship of such an occasion. This provides an opportunity for mothers to become acquainted with one another and with the nursery class leaders.

Although the colored Easter egg has come to us from pagan sources, the egg is universally a symbol of life, and as such is not out of place in the celebration of Easter. We do not, of course, use any symbols with three-year-olds. Gaily-colored Easter eggs are enjoyed for the fun they may give.

Throughout the year we try to get parents to dress their children simply and comfortably in clothes which wash easily and are not damaged by sitting on the floor. At Easter time, the children are likely to be self-conscious about new clothing. They will be eager to show it to us and tell us about it. We should admire the new clothes and may comment that it is good to have thoughtful mothers and fathers who love us and provide clothes for us to wear.

Since many more parents come to church at Easter than at any other time, the nursery class will be crowded. Many churches having double or triple worship services, will also have double or triple nursery class sessions. Some of the children may be total strangers. It is wise to have additional adult helpers and to plan with special care to prevent confusion and to insure a happy session.

Before you begin making preparations for April sessions in the nursery class, read *My Book for Spring,* both the stories for the children and messages for adults who use the book. Read the suggestions for the observance of Easter and the suggested teacher helps for the entire quarter in this text. Study carefully the notes in *Child Guidance in Christian Living* for April. Every worker in the class for three-year-olds should do this, not just the leading teacher. A workers' meeting to evaluate the work of the preceding quarter, to make plans for the quarter just beginning, to consider the individual development and needs of the children, and to share the physical and social work of getting the room ready for spring will prove most helpful.

Copies of *My Book for Spring* should be secured several weeks before the beginning of the new quarter. Get several extra copies to use for clipping songs, pictures, and stories for mounting on cardboard for special use. Place several copies in various centers of activity so that they may be reached for and used whenever opportunity arises. Each teacher should be sufficiently familiar with the stories to be able to share the main idea of each in conversation with children at any time. The teachers should also learn any new songs.

Prepare each child's book with his name. Every worker should sign the letters on pages 2 and 3. If enrollment is increasing, you may need to secure an additional worker. If so, mention this in a note to parents and introduce the new leader to the children. Remember that men make excellent workers with three-year-olds. Be sure to provide a teacher's text and pupil's book for any new workers.

If the copies of *My Book for Spring* are given out just before Easter, you may enclose a personal note or mimeographed letter to parents, telling them of your plans for observing Easter in the class for three-year-olds. Books may be given to the children as they meet their parents at the door of the classroom. If any child receives this as his first book, it should be taken to him on a visit to his home. After two Sundays, any books not yet given out should be delivered to the child at home.

April

Possible Stories for April (select from these stories in *My Book for Spring*, Part 3): "Jesus Tells About God's Care," "The Rainy Day," "Our Minister Comes to Nursery Class," "A Visit to the Sanctuary."

Possible Songs for April: "Friends at Church," "Jesus Saw the Flowers," "My Friends," "When I'm Very Happy," "Spring Is Here," "Pitter Patter," "Sing, O Sing," "Teeter-Totter."

Possible Pictures for April: "Jesus Tells About God's Care" and "A Rainy Day," from *Nursery Class Pictures.* See also page 153.

Possible Activities for April: Talk about Easter flowers. Play matching dresses and suits with the colors of the flowers. Watch for evidence of spring. Watch the rain. Feel the rain on hands or faces. Enjoy feeding fish or bird. Enjoy visit of minister. Listen to spring records. Play simple games. Visit the sanctuary.

My Picture Card: Select from April, May, June.

APRIL IS A SPRING MONTH IN MOST OF OUR COUNTRY. CHILDREN who are three enjoy every evidence of spring that they find. We are privileged to share their wonder at beauty and evidences of new life all about us. Often there is rainy weather this month. This may mean many days indoors. The children are likely to be restless and to appear noisy. It may be wise to plan for more quiet play and encourage the children to use "indoor voices." But many days will be beautiful and in every area there will be much to enjoy, wonder at, and cause us to worship.

Throughout the year, when children speak in loud tones it is well to remind them to use their quiet voices indoors. Sometimes a teacher may say, "When you use such a loud voice, I cannot understand you. Save your loud voice for outdoors. Now tell me again what you wish to say." Usually this results in a lower tone.

Purpose

To think of Jesus as a man who loved birds and flowers; to continue to direct children's appreciation for the beauties of new life in spring and the benefits of spring rain; to help them achieve a happy rela-

151

tionship with the minister; to help them begin to appreciate the beauty of the church sanctuary.

Suggested Bible Study for Teachers

Read Genesis 8:22; Job 5:8-10; 36:26 through 37:16; Psalms 104. Think of God the creator who planned for day and night, for heat and cold, for rain and sunshine. Consider the joy that is ours as recipients of His bountiful love. We will not use these or similar passages of Scripture with young children, but as we grow in our own recognition of God the creator, of an orderly universe of his planning, of ourselves as his highest creation, our own love should be strengthened. The more closely we live to God, the more certainly will we reveal him to the children whom we teach.

As we try to help boys and girls accept responsibility for providing care for birds and to come to know and have a happy relationship with their minister, we will do well to read Paul's letter to the Ephesians. Study particularly Ephesians 4. Think of your minister as one who is called of God to serve him. Consider your own gifts and privileges of service as a calling from God, also. Are you serving in that spirit? If not, perhaps therein lies the explanation for any impatience and failure. You have cause to be grateful that the church has given you the responsibility and opportunity to have a part in the developing religious life of its children during one of the most important years of childhood.

Preparations for April Sessions

Be sure that your classroom is clean, bright, and attractive. Fresh paint may be needed for the walls or new curtains for the windows. Some new materials and play equipment may need to be added. It may be possible to secure these from your children's division council and commission on education. You may decide to rearrange the room in order to use each center of activity to the greatest advantage. In planning such rearrangement remember that children find security in the familiar. It is suggested, therefore, that not too many changes be made in the room.

Check outdoor space used by the children. If there is a playground, be sure that fence and equipment are in good condition. If you have had no outdoor space, this may be the time to make an effort to secure some. Even a very small space in which to dig and plant seeds may be very helpful. If going outdoors during the Sunday sessions is impossible, you and your children may continue looking out the windows. If your view is not attractive, you may be able to do something about making it so. One church nursery class in a beautiful city had windows overlooking a drive at the back of the church. Garbage disposal and ash cans were kept directly opposite the nursery classroom windows. When these were removed and shrubbery planted in that spot, the entire outlook was greatly improved.

Have ready the pictures, "Jesus Tells About God's Care" and "A Rainy Day." The pictures of spring flowers and planting experiences used in March may be left in the room. Add others showing rainy day experiences, the minister, and the children in the church sanctuary.

Have ready a large piece of brown paper, approximately 36x24 inches cut in the shape of a mud puddle, for dramatic play.

If someone can be responsible for bringing an aquarium with fish or a canary or parakeet in a cage, it might be placed where the children can enjoy it. Have fish and bird food available.

Bring in flowering shrubs and flowers.

Make arrangements for the minister to visit the group and what time he is to arrive. Ask him to stay for at least ten minutes so that all the children who wish to do so may have an opportunity to share their toys or sing together for the minister. Be sure to invite him to become one of the group, not to talk to the children.

Plan a visit to the sanctuary. Before taking the children, teachers should go into the sanctuary together and discuss ways of making a visit there worthwhile for the children. Perhaps you will notice picture windows about which you should be prepared to comment or answer questions. You may arrange to have the organist play for you when you come. If you wish to have the organist accompany the children when they sing, you will arrange this before the session and provide music for the song, "Friends at Church" or "When I'm Very Happy." You may notice pools of color on the floor as sunlight filters through stained glass windows. Perhaps the minister may meet you there. If he wears a robe for adult services, children will be interested in seeing him with it on. Perhaps they will be interested in touching it. Be sure that each child knows the minister's name.

If you have a bulletin board near your classroom door, arrange it attractively, using at least one picture, a bit of poetry, and some information concerning your plans for Easter. Sample copies of leaflets to be given to parents may be displayed. (See page 148.)

If you do not have a parents' meeting, at least send home a letter explaining how the nursery class will celebrate Easter and why. Enclose one or two of the leaflets mentioned. Reread "Parents of Nursery Class Children," page 38.

You may wish to provide a pansy plant in a small pot for each child to take home on Easter.

Have available the music records, "To a Wild Rose," "To a Water Lily," or "Spring Song" for a listening time.

Turn to "The Nursery Class Teacher," page 32. In what ways have you grown as a teacher since last October? What books have you read to improve your techniques? Read pages 151 through 176.

SUGGESTED PROCEDURE

FIRST SUNDAY

This session is for Easter. When Easter falls on the second, third, or fourth Sunday of April, use these suggestions on Easter Sunday. Substitute the suggestions for another Sunday for today's plans.

As the children arrive, greet them with "A Happy Easter." It is especially necessary today to have the children wear name tags. Mention but do not dwell on their new clothes.

If children bring Easter baskets, toy rabbits, colored eggs, or candy, suggest that after showing them to others, they place them on a shelf above the rack where their wraps are hung for safe keeping until time to go home. Large safety pins, or clip clothespins may be used to clip hats, gloves, purses, and so on, to the owner's coat. More than likely there will be so many new things that if some system is not worked out, there will be confusion in finding wraps and purses. Call attention to the Easter flowers that you have in the room. It is fun to match dresses and suits with the colors of the flowers.

Without rushing them, help the children find something interesting to do. This may include building with blocks, playing in the housekeeping center, enjoying books and pictures, looking out the window, listening to recorded music, sharing a singing time at the piano, looking at flowers, young green leaves, and other beautiful things which say that spring is coming (or is here). It is likely that there has been egg hunting or other confusion at home this morning. Try to provide a calm, happy atmosphere for the entire session.

If flowers were planted, note their growth and water them. If bulbs were planted last fall, some blooms may be enjoyed this session. Should you have a tulip tree, japonica, or other flowering tree or bush in the church yard, provide an opportunity for the children to see it. This will be a time for a thank-you prayer.

If every worker in the room is alert to opportunities for doing so, most of the children should hear the story, "Jesus Tells About God's Care," *My Book for Spring*, page 6, at least once during the session.

The children will also enjoy looking at the picture of Jesus. Try to help them to feel, "This is Easter Day. It is a happy day." In some situations it may be possible to take the children, a few at a time, to see the flowers in the sanctuary. Sing "Jesus Saw the Flowers," page 225.

Any other stories or songs used should be those in keeping with the season and the ideas which teachers are trying to share on the Sundays preceding and following Easter.

As children leave tell them that you are glad to have shared this happy Easter Day with them. If new children have come, be sure that their names and addresses are correctly recorded in order that you may get in touch with them, invite them to come regularly, and provide each with a copy of *My Book for Spring*. If it is the custom to provide a potted pansy plant for each child, this may be given as the children leave. If possible, let each child decide what color pansy plant he wishes.

Give each child *My Picture Card*, Number 1. Be careful to give this card, planned for Easter, on Easter Day. This may make it necessary to rearrange the cards since Easter is a changeable date.

SECOND SUNDAY

(If possible use these suggestions on a rainy Sunday. Rearrange suggestions for April as necessary.)

As the children arrive, greet them as before. Since this session is planned for a rainy day, it may be that the suggestions included will be used on some other Sunday when it is raining. If the weather is fair today, use the suggestions for some other Sunday this month. Mention the rain as you help children remove raincoats, caps, and boots. Suggest that several of them join you in looking out the window, calling attention to grass, trees, flowers, and shrubs which look fresh and green because of the showers. Remind the children that the rain is giving a drink to the seeds they planted outdoors. Just watching the raindrops splash in the puddles or on the sidewalks makes good conversation. Sing "Pitter Patter," page 222. If possible, open the window and let the children feel the rain on their hands or faces. This may lead to a brief thank-you prayer.

Look at the picture, "A Rainy Day." Talk about the goodness of fathers and mothers who supply us with clothing to protect us from the rain. Make up a song about what to do on a rainy day, such as

> Janie came to church school
>   on a rainy Sunday,
> She wore a raincoat and rubber boots
>   on a rainy Sunday.
> Janie played with Susan.
> She played with Tommy, too.
> Janie had a happy time
>   on a rainy Sunday.

Reread "Music in the Nursery Class," page 71 of this book, for suggestions concerning how to make up songs.

The children may play that they are getting ready to go out in the rain. They will pretend to put on their rubbers and storm coats and to raise an umbrella. Use the brown paper cut in the shape of a mud puddle or a chalk mark drawn on the bare floor or linoleum for dramatic play. The children may have the fun of showing how they walk around the edge of a mud puddle. Reference may be made to the fact that boys and girls who remember to walk around mud puddles are big enough to help care for themselves.

In helping children to stay busy and happy, you will need to guide them to find something interesting to do, and to make changes from time to time. Three-year-olds do not always know when they need to change from quiet interests to active play or from active to quiet occupations. A suggestion from an alert teacher may prevent overexertion or boredom.

The story, "The Rainy Day," *My Book for Spring*, page 8, may be told over and over. *It's Springtime* by Lois Lenski, may be added to the book center and used throughout the spring season.

Prayers for a rainy day session may be, "Dear God, we are glad that you planned for sunshine and rain," or "We are glad to see the rain," or "We are glad to see the grass and flowers grow after the rain."

Some children may enjoy listening to the record player. Others may gather at the piano to sing "Pitter Patter," page 222, "Spring Is Here," page 220 or "God's Care," page 224.

Puzzles, play with floor toys, housekeeping play, and other quiet activities should be encouraged as usual. Active play, such as building with large blocks, rocking in the boat, climbing, and jumping will give children an opportunity to stretch muscles and work off energy.

Times of active play should be followed by a few moments of quiet before children find other activities.

As the children leave, remind them to show their picture card (Number 2) to their fathers and mothers.

THIRD SUNDAY

As the children arrive, greet them as usual. Put on name tags again today. Call attention to the spring flowers. The children may again enjoy matching the colors of the flowers with their dresses and suits. The pictures in the room will be of interest, also. The large picture, "Jesus Tells About God's Care," may be in evidence. If the children show interest, tell the story.

Sing "Flowers," tune, "Church," page 224, substituting the word "flowers" for "church." You may also sing "Spring Is Here," page 220.

This may be an appropriate time to pray, "Dear God, when we see flowers, they help us to remember that you love us. We are glad that Jesus told about the birds and flowers. Amen."

There may be continued interest in the care of the outdoor garden or window box. In some parts of the country the bulbs planted last fall may just be blooming. Whenever this happens, go out to see them.

If a bowl of fish, or a bird in a cage has been provided for today, share the children's interest in these living things. One or two children may feed the fish or bird. Talk of ways of caring for them, including being quiet, keeping our hands off them, and not frightening them. Sing "God's Care," page 224.

The leader may explain to the children as she moves around the room that Dr. ———————, our minister, is coming to visit us today. He would like to see the dolls, the blocks, the books. He would like to see us take turns on the rocking boat or slide. Suggest that children in the housekeeping center clean house to get ready for the minister. Suggest that those who are working puzzles or looking at books, show him the pictures. Mention that we are wearing tags so that our minister will know each of us by name.

When the minister comes lead him from group to group, introducing him to the children. Many will already know him. Some children will be eager to say hello to him. Move away from the group with whom he is visiting and permit him to become acquainted with the children. If his personality is such that he would enjoy doing so, encourage him to sit on a low chair or on the floor, joining the children in their activities.

After a little while with one group, you may suggest that he move over to another group to become acquainted. The children who have built with the blocks may show him what they have made. Some may like to sing one or two favorite songs. If there are flowers blooming in the garden or window box, one may be given to the minister when he leaves. Tell him that you hope he will come again soon.

Tell the story, "Our Minister Comes to Nursery Class," *My Book for Spring,* page 13, to as many of the children as seem interested. Sing, "My Friends," page 219, using the phrase, "our minister." You may also sing "Friends at Church," page 214, mentioning the fact that Dr. ———— is one of our friends at church.

When the children leave, tell them that you enjoyed seeing them and will be looking for them next Sunday. Give each child his copy of *My Picture Card,* Number 3. Remind him to show it to Mother and Father.

FOURTH SUNDAY

As the children arrive, have name tags ready for each. Help each child to find something to do.

At the book center, have ready the books, *Jesus, the Children's Friend, It's Springtime,* and books about birds and animals.

Looking out the window for signs of spring and looking at flowers in a bowl in the room will provide opportunities for talking about the beauty of springtime. Sing the song, "Sing, O Sing," page 222, and "Spring Is Here," page 220.

Suggest that one or several children enjoy songs and quiet music with the pianist or at the record player. If you have such records as "To a Wild Rose," "To a Water Lily," or "Spring Song," you may mention that the persons who made up this music were thinking about spring flowers. Encourage children to listen quietly.

Play "Sing, O Sing" from *My Book* Nursery Album as the children listen. Since three-year-olds have a very short interest span, you will not expect them to sit or stand quietly for very long at a time. Children may come and go from such a listening group. You may wish to intersperse quiet music with rhythms or marches to which you clap hands, tap feet on the floor, or tap sticks together. The children may enjoy singing.

Games are not organized with three-year-olds. They simply begin as a teacher takes one or two children by the hand, forms a small circle and begins to play. You may play one of the games played before or enjoy "Teeter-Totter," page 208.

Be sure that at least one worker is available to tell the story, "A Visit to the Sanctuary," *My Book for Spring,* page 16, to any child who wishes to listen.

Show a picture of people in the church sanctuary. Speak to the children of the part of the church where fathers and mothers go to hear the minister talk to them about God. Tell the children that they are going to see this part of our church together. Tell them that this part of the church is called the sanctuary.

Before going to the sanctuary, suggest that toys be picked up and put away. Invite small groups of four or five children at a time. A leader will go with each group. The children in each group will hold the walking tape. (See page 67.)

Some children may prefer to remain in the room. If so, a worker should stay with them. As each group reaches the entrance to the sanctuary, let the children walk in without holding to the tape. Stop at the entrance and remind them that in this part of our church, we are quiet. We walk carefully. We may ask questions. We will look at the beautiful windows. While in the sanctuary, if no other group is meeting there, sing, "Friends at Church," page 214, or "When I'm Very Happy," page 223.

If previous arrangements are made with the organist, the children may listen to organ music. This should be only a three to five-minute listening time.

In the sanctuary, depend upon the beauty of the place, the music of the organ, and your own attitude to help children feel its bigness, its beauty, and the worshipful atmosphere. You may wish to sit down in the front pews and look around. After a few moments you may call the children's attention to the big Bible and to any window you particularly wish them to see. Talk about the sun shining through the colored windows. If the glass is clear, encourage the children to tell what they see.

Perhaps you will plan to show the offering plates. Explain that some of the fathers take these offering plates to the other mothers and fathers who put their money in these plates just as the girls and boys put their money in the plate or dish or basket in the nursery class.

If the minister can meet you, suggest that he wear his robe and that he tell the children that this is the robe he wears when he talks to the mothers and fathers and other persons in church on Sunday.

Before leaving the sanctuary, say, "Thank you, God, for our church. Thank you for our minister. Amen." If the organist has played for you, be sure to include him in your prayer, also.

Return quietly to the nursery classroom. Give out the copies of *My Picture Card*, Number 4, to take home and remind each child to tell Mother and Father about the visit to the sanctuary.

FIFTH SUNDAY

When April or May has five Sundays, use suggestions for the fifth Sunday in June, page 175, and give *My Picture Card*, Number 13.

May

POSSIBLE MATERIALS AND ACTIVITIES

Possible Stories for May (select from these stories in *My Book for Spring*, Part 3): "A Home for Baby Birds," "Helping Mother," "In Our Garden," "John's Policeman Friend."

Possible Songs for May: "Spring Is Here," "Sing, O Sing," "Helping Mother," "The Redbird," "Friends at Church."

Possible Picture for May: "Jesus Tells About God's Care," from *Nursery Class Pictures.*

Possible Activities for May: Walks to look for signs of spring. Play flying around like birds. Listen to records. Play simple games. Play ways of helping at home.

My Picture Card: Select from April, May, June.

IF SCHOOLS CLOSE EARLY IN YOUR AREA AND YOUR CHURCH STARTS its vacation church school program for children in May or June, turn now and read the discussion of vacation church school activities for three-year-olds, page 89. All workers should read the suggestions for the entire month of May and become familiar with the stories planned for use so that they can tell them briefly at any time. Learn the songs and become familiar with the pictures. Read the section for workers with three-year-olds in the May issue of *Child Guidance in Christian Living.* This may be the basis for your discussion at your planning session for this month. As usual, you will also plan specific responsibilities.

Participate in your church observance of Christian Family Week. Arrange your bulletin board to emphasize the idea of family influence upon the development of Christian character. Share leaflets on religion in the home with parents. (See page 148.) Encourage parents to call upon you for any special help you may be able to give in guiding children.

Purpose

To help children become aware of the pleasures of home and family life and to continue to appreciate the beauties of nature and to associate them with God's plan for the world.

Suggested Bible Study for Teachers

Read both of Paul's letters to his young friend Timothy. As they are short, each of them may be read through at a sitting. Note particularly in the second letter, Paul's references to the home life of Timothy. Think of the influence the mother and grandmother exerted upon this young man. Keep in mind that, while we who teach in the church school are privileged to make a contribution to the religious development of the children, the child's parents and others of his family are his most important teachers of religion.

Preparations for May Sessions

Check all equipment for cleanliness and safety.

Be sure that all doll clothing, table and bed covers are clean. Have ready an extra supply of sheets and blankets for doll beds.

Clip and mount pictures from *My Book for Spring*.

Have brooms, dustpan, dust cloths, and other clean-up material in housekeeping center.

Check growing plants and blooming flowers.

Provide a few fancy hats, high heeled shoes, and purses for dramatic play. Also have a man's hat.

Add new puzzles, related to family activities if possible.

Arrange to have fresh flowers in your room each Sunday. Place these in low bowls or small vases. Three-year-olds like to feel the texture and smell the flowers, as well as look at them. It is well to let the children help fill the bowl or vase with water and arrange the flowers.

Secure pictures and books about birds, flowers, and children helping at home.

Cut a bird from colored construction paper for each child. Have ready small safety pins. You may prefer to paste a colored bird seal on a white card for the children to wear.

Secure a bird house or nest, a few feathers, bits of colored wool.

For Mother's Day, prepare a folder for each child to take home to mother. Place inside the following poem,

> Thank you, God, for Mother,
> Who works and plays with me.
> We sing and we tell stories,
> As happy as can be.

If you plan to take the children on a walk, go over the route in advance so that you will not waste time on Sunday morning in finding a flower garden. If you plan to sit on the grass, provide a rug or quilt.

If you plan to have a policeman visit, tell him the purpose of his visit and what time he is to arrive. Ask him to bring his cap and whistle. Request him not to show or mention his gun unless a child asks him about it. Then he will explain that the gun is not often used. Read again, "Visitors," page 67.

Make a large drawing of a traffic light. Paste red and green paper on it for use in dramatic play.

Reread "The Three-Year-Old," page 15, and "Some Special Problems," page 22.

SUGGESTED PROCEDURE

FIRST SUNDAY

Greet the children as they arrive, commenting on the beauty of the day. Suggest that money for the church be put into the container. Say that it is good to have families who give us money for the church.

Have on hand the colored birds cut from construction paper. Let each child choose a bird. Write his or her name on it. Use a safety pin to fasten the bird on each child. Say, "You may take this home with you to show Father and Mother."

Help children to find something to do.

Pictures and books will provide opportunities to talk and enjoy stories and songs, such as "Sing, O Sing," page 222, "Spring Is Here," page 220, and "The Redbird," page 218. There may be opportunities to say a thank-you prayer for flowers and birds.

By this time of year, several of the children will be four years old or nearly so, and having been in the nursery class for a year, will be ready for more and longer stories. They will enjoy a greater number of songs. As other children will be coming to the nursery class throughout the year when they reach their third birthdays, teachers will be concerned to meet the different needs of each group, as well as to continue to have happy sessions as the number of children in the class grows. In most situations, teachers will meet the problems due to differences in age and development by planning for individual and small group activities on various levels of development.

The younger children will continue to play alone, though enjoying being near other children. Older children may enjoy more group play, singing games, and shared activity in building, dramatizing family life, and so on. Workers will need to watch carefully in order to meet the needs of each group without trespassing on the rights of the other.

Other activities which may be enjoyed include outdoor play or walks to look for signs of spring; putting water in the birdbath; such indoor fun as painting with damp colored chalk; cleaning house; block building; play with trucks and autos, working puzzles; group games, as "Ring-Rosy," "Teeter-Totter," "Get Acquainted Game," and so on.

The children will be interested in looking at birds' nests, a bird house, a few feathers, and the bird pictures. Call special attention to these, speaking of the way in which God has caused each bird to know how to build a nest and that not all nests are alike.

Sing the bird song. Perhaps, as the pianist plays, some of the children may wish to play that they are birds. After flying around a few children may "roost" on the walking board to hear the story, "A Home for Baby Birds," *My Book for Spring*, page 21. Sing "The Redbird," page 218. Say a prayer of gladness for birds and flowers. Children who heard the story may enjoy going outside and placing bits of colored wool on bushes and shrubs as Randy did in the story.

Open the Bible and repeat "Birds of the air have nests" (Matthew 8:20). Tell the children that those words are in the Bible. Use the large picture, "Jesus Tells About God's Care."

As the children leave, remind them to show father and mother the birds they are wearing and to tell their parents about the picture on *My Picture Card*, Number 5.

SECOND SUNDAY

As the children arrive they may say, "This is my Mother's Day." Comment to them on how good it is to have Mother who loves and cares for us. If some children live with grandmothers or other persons who take their mother's place, mention this person specifically, or by the title by which she is known to the child. Suggest that money which is placed in the offering container is used to help some children to have a happy home.

Permit those who wish to play alone, to do so without bothering them.

As other children find things to do, you may offer suggestions in the various centers as follows:

Suggest that children at the block center build houses and play families with Wedgie or Rubber Play People. Talk about families living together in homes.

Suggest that the children in the housekeeping center clean house, hang clothes on the line, or dress up and play Mother and children. Show pictures of children helping at home. Some may play ways in which they help mother at home. This would be similar to "Getting Ready for Nursery Class" page 208, substituting such ideas as "This is the way I put away toys," or "This is the way I sweep the walk," or "This is the way I dry the dishes," and so on. During this game or during housekeeping or doll play, there may be opportunities for a short prayer, such as "Thank you, God, for mothers and little babies" or "Thank you, God, for mothers. We like to help mother." Sing "Helping Mother," page 223.

Other children may play with clay, work puzzles, or look at books and pictures. A few may enjoy listening to a record or singing at the piano.

Encourage children to examine objects of beauty outdoors, or brought in from outside, noting particularly any growth or blooming of flowers in their garden.

If you have outdoor space, some of the older children may play such games as "Ring-Rosy," "Teeter-Totter" or "Getting Ready for Nursery Class," pages 207 and 208.

Stay near by to insure safe play with big muscle equipment.

Sing the suggested songs as the opportunity arises.

Several small groups may hear the story, "Helping Mother," *My Book for Spring,* page 24.

Give each child a folder. (See page 162.) Suggest that they give their mothers (or the person who takes the mother's place) this pretty folder which their teachers have made. Number 6 is the card for today.

After the Session

Have you told and retold the stories most needed by your children? Not all stories in their books have been mentioned in the plans for the sessions. Each teacher will tell the stories where they will best fit.

Are you using opportunities to sing informally as the children play? How often in the past month have you offered a brief prayer with a small group? Are you availing yourself of opportunities for your own spiritual growth?

THIRD SUNDAY

As the children come, express appreciation for mothers and fathers who bring them to nursery class. Money will be put into the offering container as usual.

If you plan to take a walk today to see flowers, each teacher who greets children as they arrive should call their attention to pretty flowers inside the room, pictures of flowers, and to any flowers they can see outside the window. As the teacher greets each child, say, "After a while, we will take a walk to see more pretty flowers blooming." Sing "Sing, O Sing," page 222, and "Church," page 224, substituting the word "flowers."

Children should be encouraged to talk about flower gardens at home. Knowing the children and their homes will make such conversation of much greater value.

If you have several kinds of flowers with foliage and petals of different textures, children will enjoy feeling and talking about these. You may repeat "Sing, O Sing" several times, mentioning each flower by name as you sing.

Take as many of the children as wish to go for a walk. Be sure that you have enough adults to go along to make such a walk safe and that children understand how and why they must stay together. If there is a flower garden or flower beds at the church, or nearby at some home, you may visit there. Enjoy a quiet time looking to see how many beautiful things you can find. Perhaps you may sit under the shade of a tree. Mention blue sky, green grass, trees, birds, and flowers.

You may play a game of colors: "I am thinking of something blue. Guess what it is." Let the children guess. (It may be the blue sky or it may be a blue flower.) Continue the game of colors as long as the children are interested. Before returning to your room, thank God for happy times together and the lovely flowers growing in the garden.

If there is time when the children return to their room, tell the story, "In Our Garden," *My Book for Spring*, page 29. Should there be no garden near enough to visit, the story will be told. If possible, it should be told outdoors, even if this means merely sitting on the church steps where the sky can be seen.

Encourage the children to dress dolls. Three-year-olds can undress dolls easily but will need help in getting the dolls dressed again. Both boys and girls should be encouraged in this activity. You may hang some of the doll clothes on the coat rack and play taking the dolls to buy new clothes. Or you may encourage the play of going to town to shop.

Continue to talk about how children help their mothers. Some may play bed-making with a teacher on one side of the doll bed and a child on the other. Show the children how to tuck sheets in at corners. The doll bed should be large enough and strong enough to permit a child to go to bed in it, if one should wish to do so. Sing "Helping Mother," page 223. Use picture clipped from *My Book*.

As the children leave, call their attention to the fact that the same story they heard today is in *My Book for Spring* which they enjoy at home. Give each child *My Picture Card*, Number 7.

FOURTH SUNDAY

As the children arrive, help each to find what he wishes to do. Perhaps some will choose the rocking boat or slide. Others may prefer a quiet activity. Some will play at the housekeeping center, some will build with blocks, others may work puzzles, enjoy plants and flowers, or go to the book center. Tell stories enjoyed previously.

Some children will continue to play alone. Others may play in small groups. No child should be urged to join a group. When he is ready he will do so of his own accord. On the other hand, help any who are shy to find a place in a small group.

Help the children think of the policeman as their friend. If there is a policeman on the corner near the church or if the leader knows that the child has to pass a policeman on the way to church school, it may be that there will be interest in talking about this experience. Some child may speak of the policeman as "catching people." In this case the leader may skillfully lead the child to realize that the policeman is a friend who likes to help. You will wish to use pictures and tell the story, "John's Policeman Friend," *My Book for Spring*, page 32.

Use the traffic light to play crossing the street. Explain that sometimes policemen (or police women) help older brothers and sisters cross the street on their way to school, even when there is a traffic light.

Children may play that they are taking walks, pushing trucks, rolling dolls in carriages, or pulling wagons. Encourage them to watch the lights, stop at the red light, and go on the green light.

One or two children may play with the small automobiles and one may be a policeman and tell them when the cars may go and when they must stop. The children will probably find their own way of playing. It will not be like the adult's understanding of policeman play but will be a satisfying learning experience for the children.

If the policeman comes into the group he may show the children his whistle just as the policeman in the story showed the whistle. The leader should confer with the policeman beforehand so that there will be no danger of his offering to let any of the children blow his whistle. This is a health precaution. We teach the children that toys are not to be put in the mouth and articles that do go in one person's mouth are not to be passed to another person. This rule should be as strictly enforced with the policeman's whistle as with any other object.

If no policeman can come into the group, but the children can see one directing traffic, they may stand at the window and watch him. Or they may put on their wraps and go out near the curb provided there is not too much traffic and that there are enough leaders to care for the children adequately.

Use the prayer, "Thank you, God, for policeman friends" or "We are glad the policemen friends help to take care of us. Thank you, God, for policemen friends."

As children leave, suggest that they tell Father and Mother about their policeman friend. Sing "Friends at Church" while the children wait for their parents, mentioning the policeman as a friend.

Give each child *My Picture Card*, Number 8.

If May has five Sundays, see page 160.

After the Session

As you consider the Christian nurture of each child, refer to your notebook in which you keep personal records of each. What growth in social behavior can you notice? Is there any greater emotional control?

Of what personal value has been the suggested Bible enrichment for the teacher? Have you read any complete series of books as suggested on page 36? Do you attend morning worship regularly?

June

POSSIBLE MATERIALS AND ACTIVITIES

Possible Stories for June (select from these stories in *My Book for Spring*, Part 3): "We Put Away Our Toys," "The Diesel Engine," "Clean Hands," "The Barber," "Good-by, Mother," "A Visit to the Sanctuary."

Possible Songs for June: "Church," "Friends at Church," "Taking Turns," "Helping Mother," "Pitter-Patter."

Possible Pictures for June: "Clean Hands," from *Nursery Class Pictures*. See also page 170.

Possible Activities for June: Enjoy dramatic play of helping at home and church. Listen to records. Play simple games. Visit the sanctuary.

My Picture Card: Select from April, May, June.

JUNE MARKS THE BEGINNING OF THE VACATION SEASON. SINCE IT will be the beginning of warm days in many areas, you will need to take precautions to prevent children from overdoing and becoming overheated. While rest periods with room darkened, mats or cots, are not considered necessary for sessions of one hour, you should plan for enough quiet times and calm activities to avoid the crossness and difficulties which develop when children are overheated and overstimulated.

In a few churches, Promotion Day is observed in June. In such situations, it is recommended that the four-year-old being promoted to the kindergarten shall continue to use nursery class material until October. This will include *My Book for Spring*, *My Book for Summer*, the *Nursery Class Pictures* and *My Picture Card*. The teachers, of course, will continue using *Christian Nurture in the Nursery Class*.

It will be well for teachers who have planned their vacation schedules to talk these over in the regular planning session. Then prepared substitutes can be ready.

Purpose

To continue the development of a sense of security through everyday experiences of children; to help the three-year-olds more fully appreciate their responsibility in putting away toys when they are through playing.

169

Suggested Bible Study for Teachers

Read 1 John, 2 John, 3 John, and Romans 8:37-39. Think of the love of God toward you and for all those who know, love, and serve Him; think of God's love for all mankind. It is interesting to realize that "God is love" comes so late in the scriptural descriptions of him when it is so perfect a definition. Discouragement, ineffectiveness, and other difficulties are eased when we accept the joyous assurance of God's love in all that we undertake to do in his service. Read the passage from Romans as a background for worship in your workers' meeting.

Preparation for June Sessions

Provide protection from glare from windows during the warm, bright days ahead.

On the first Sunday the toys and other materials may be left on the shelves or in boxes.

Continue to have fresh flowers for the room. Notice especially the use made of them on the third Sunday. Small vases and pitchers of water will also be needed.

Have on hand pictures and books showing children putting away toys, washing hands, visiting a barber, a Diesel engine pulling a train. Some of these pictures may be those clipped from one copy of the children's books and mounted ready for use.

Be sure that all toys and equipment are in good repair. If a good floor train has not been part of your equipment, try to get one. Small wooden boxes, fastened together with cup hooks and screw eyes, may be substituted but a large floor train is preferable.

SUGGESTED PROCEDURE

FIRST SUNDAY

As the children come, greet them, and speak of how nice it is to see church friends again. Sing "Church Bells," page 214.

Permit children to enjoy play in the various activity centers with a minimum of suggestions. They may be encouraged to get out their own toys. Use opportunities for stressing the greater responsibilities that the children in the nursery class have now that they are growing bigger.

Talk about being big enough to do many things. Be specific.

Recall ways in which they help at home, such as drying silver, helping to make beds, bringing in newspaper and mail from the porch, with special emphasis on being big enough to remember to put toys away when they have finished playing with them. This idea will be emphasized at each of the interest centers. Say, "When you put a toy back where it belongs when you have finished, then another child can find it to use."

Throughout the sessions, teachers will pick up and put away toys scattered about and should encourage children to do so. It would be pleasant to have a neat orderly room when the children leave, but if everything is put away at a given time or signal, children whose parents do not come for them immediately are likely to be disturbed. Rather, encourage a general practice of cleaning up and of being orderly in care of toys and other materials. This is the sort of thing which must be worked at continually.

Tell the story, "We Put Away Our Toys," *My Book for Spring,* page 40, to small groups who are interested. Repeat the verse,

> "We are growing bigger, stronger
> We can do things by ourselves,
> We can put away our toys
> We can put blocks on the shelves" [1]

There may be opportunities to offer a prayer of thanks for big girls and boys who are learning to put toys away.

Several children may enjoy singing. Words of several songs should be familiar by now. One favorite will probably be "Taking Turns," page 221. Listening to records may be enjoyed, too.

If possible, go outdoors to play. If the space is limited and you do not have equipment, you may play a few games outdoors. If you have a well-equipped playground, you will find many opportunities for singing "Taking Turns" and "Friends at Church," pages 221, 214.

Instead of singing "Taking Turns," you may repeat a suggestion in rhythmic fashion, such as "Up the ladder and down the slide, we know how to take turns." Or, "I'll take my place at the end of the line and wait to have another turn." Since three-year-olds often sing in a monotone, such repetition, when spoken is as effective as singing. The teacher who cannot sing, can chant, or speak the words on the notes. Inside equipment may be used in the same way, chant-

[1] Rosemary K. Roorbach.

ing or speaking about the rocking boat, ladder, slide, blocks, and so on.

As the children leave, be sure that each has *My Picture Card,* Number 9.

SECOND SUNDAY

After greeting the children, encourage them to follow their own interests—play with puzzles, floor toys, and blocks.

Housekeeping play may continue as before. There will be increased interest in the floor train, especially if a big one is available.

The children will enjoy looking at the pictures of engines.

If a story is used today, tell "The Diesel Engine," *My Book for Spring,* page 37, to small groups of children who are interested. The story may be told at the book center, to children who play with toys on the floor, and to children in the housekeeping center.

Use songs and prayer as opportunities arise.

Suggest taking a train trip. Make a train with the walking board, the rocking boat, or rows of chairs. Speak of a train as a train, of the engine as a Diesel engine. If you imitate the sound of a train as part of playing a game with a group of children, make a humming sound, with some click-clacking and a whooing sound for the whistle. If you play train with a rocking boat, remind both passengers and crew that the train must be standing still when people get off and on. Let one child be the engineer. Encourage children to tell where they would like to go and to talk of trips they have taken.

If any of the children are taking trips in the near future, wish them a pleasant time as they leave today. Be sure to speak to the parents about taking the child's book on the trip and enjoying it with him. Mention also that both parents will be reading the sections written for them. Give each child *My Picture Card,* Number 10.

THIRD SUNDAY

Welcome the children as they come. If there are those who have been on trips, they will be eager to tell about their travels. Some may describe an airplane trip, "Way up in the clouds." A few may tell about going to bed on the train. Probably most of them will report on an automobile trip. Some of the older children may play going on a trip using the form of transportation which was used by the family.

The flowers which the teacher brought should be on papers on a low table. After conversation about vacations, ask several children to help arrange the flowers in small vases. Encourage the children to fill the vases with water from pitchers that the leader has ready for them. They may arrange the flowers carefully. Then the children may be taken to the washroom where they may wash their hands by themselves under supervision. During conversation about washing hands, the leader may draw the children's attention to the large picture and story, "Clean Hands," *My Book for Spring*, page 45. Perhaps there will be a request for this story. If so, it may be told. The children will be encouraged to wash their hands carefully just as Becky did. Emphasis will be placed on boys and girls being big enough to wash their hands carefully.

Children will continue play at the various interest centers as before.

After the children have followed their own interests, there may be an opportunity for them to skip in the room. Then the pianist may play softly while the children come to their resting rug or mat. A lullaby may be played softly on the piano or a record player.

If there are trees just outside the window in the nursery classroom, the children may lie on the floor and watch the leaves through the open windows. They may listen to the birds chirping or they may see the shadows of the leaves on the windows or on the wall. Perhaps they will talk together about these leaf pictures as they rest. Where trees and birds cannot be seen, music may be enjoyed.

If this is a rainy Sunday, the children may listen to the rain. The music of "Pitter Patter," page 222, may recall the words of the song to them. "We are glad for play time. We are glad, too, for rest time. Thank you, God" or "Thank you, God, for friends and play time. Thank you for rest time" are suggested prayers.

Three-year-olds will need teacher help in picking up and putting toys away before leaving with their parents.

In some parts of the country the children will be accustomed to hearing the adults' farewell with the added invitation, "Come back" or "Hurry back." Little children will imitate this and the friendly courtesy will be extended almost as a habit. The nursery leader may help to encourage this friendly behavior as she uses a similar type of farewell. As the children leave the nursery class each Sunday she has probably said, "Good-by, Joyce. I'll see you next Sunday." "Good-by, Harry, I'll see you next Sunday."

Call attention to the picture on *My Picture Card,* Number 11.

FOURTH SUNDAY

Suggest that the children put their money into the container provided for it as soon as they arrive. Remind them that the money helps pay for our electric lights, for our books, and that some of it helps other boys and girls to have a church.

Help each child to find something to do. Sing songs and tell stories as they seem to be suited to the children's interests.

A few children with a teacher may take a picture walk around the room. As children go from one picture to another, comment on each and sing an appropriate song.

Tell the story, "The Barber," *My Book for Spring,* page 48, to small groups of interested children. Let them enjoy the picture from *My Book for Spring* which will be cut from the book and mounted.

Show the picture of the little girl having her hair trimmed that is on page 50. Encourage conversation.

The leader will need to safeguard the children from any danger of experimental play of barber. She will seek to build up a feeling of friendliness toward this person and will hope to have the children think of the visit to the barber as a pleasant experience rather than one to be dreaded because of the feel of the cold scissors against the neck or the tickle of the hair as it falls. On the other hand, she does not want to make it such an interesting occasion that the children may decide to play barber at home. The teacher may say, "Only grown persons who really know how can cut our hair so that it looks nice. Sometimes Mother or Daddy will cut it. Sometimes the barber will cut it, but always a grown person does it." The children may wish to tell of their experiences in going to the barber, or they may have been in the barber shop with Daddy when his hair was trimmed, or have gone to the beauty parlor with Mother when her hair was trimmed or when she had a shampoo and set.

The children will have been encouraged to follow their usual procedure. There should be opportunities for singing together and for prayer. They may enjoy playing "Going to the Barber." In the song they may substitute the words, "This is the way my hair is washed," "This is the way I wear the towel," "This is the way I sit up straight," "This is the way my hair is combed," and so on. It is not suggested that the leader have anything depicting the way the barber cuts the hair as it is better to avoid all suggestions of the children cutting hair. There will probably be the usual interest in block building, rolling the ball, looking at the books.

Encourage the children to listen to records, gather at the piano to hear songs played and sung, or to join in singing.

Follow active play with a time of sitting quietly on the floor, listening to music on the record player.

As the children leave, the teacher may touch each child's head and remark, "I like the way the barber fixed your hair." Give each child *My Picture Card*, Number 12, and ask him to find the same picture in his book at home.

FIFTH SUNDAY

As usual, the leader will be guided by the needs of the children. If it is possible, arrange for the children to visit the sanctuary again today. When the children visit the sanctuary, the leader will plan to call their attention to a greater number of interests than they have noticed previously.

When they go to the sanctuary, the leader will pause just outside the door and remind the children that they always go into this part of the church quietly, that they may ask questions, they may look all around, but they will keep their voices low when they talk.

Perhaps some of the children have recently been baptized or a young brother or sister may have been baptized. The leader will arrange to have water placed in the font before the visit. Let the children feel the water. Then a simple explanation may be given. "Many fathers and mothers bring their babies or little children to church on a special day. The fathers and mothers carry the children to the minister. Then the minister takes the little baby in his arms and puts just a few drops of water on the baby's head as he says the baby's name. Then all the people know that this church is the baby's church as well as his parents' church."

Call attention again to the colored windows and the soft cushions, the high benches and to the place where the minister stands when he talks to the mothers and fathers. The children may be interested in the organ and may ask about it. If possible, the organist may play for them. Call attention to the Bible. The leader can explain briefly, "The Bible is the book from which the minister reads stories about Jesus. Some are the same stories that you hear in our nursery class."

Before leaving the sanctuary, use a prayer, such as "Thank you, God, for little babies. We are glad that little babies and girls and boys and fathers and mothers may all come to church."

After the visit to the sanctuary the children may play informally. If a story is requested or needed, tell either "A Visit to the Sanctuary" or "Good-by, Mother," *My Book for Spring,* pages 16 or 53.

The leader will be aware constantly that there are many more plans suggested for each Sunday than she is likely to use and that she may wish to vary the suggested procedures to meet the needs of her group. She will decide which activities are of greatest value for the children and will develop these.

Dismiss as usual, reminding the children, "Be sure to tell Daddy and Mother what we talked about when we visited the sanctuary this morning," or "Remember to tell Grandmother about when you were a baby and Mother and Daddy brought you to be baptized." (This remark will be suited to each child's experience.) *My Picture Card,* Number 13, will be given to each child.

SUMMER QUARTER

BEFORE MAKING SPECIFIC PLANS FOR EACH SUNDAY SESSION, EACH worker should read the teacher's helps for the entire quarter. She should read the pupil's book, *My Book for Summer*, including the suggestions for adults who share the book with a child. Each month, everyone who works with three-year-olds should read the pages concerning the work of this group in *Child Guidance in Christian Living*.

It is not expected that any group shall do all of the things suggested. Nor should any child participate in all of the activities that may be carried on in any one session. Rather, every worker should read all of the material, then use whatever suggestions are helpful as she works with individual children or several at one time. All workers will do some teaching.

Each child will participate in some guided activities; hear some stories, songs, and prayers; share some conversations; look at pictures, books, and nature objects. If this is done, each child should be helped to have happy times without being overcrowded with adult attention, should acquire some skills in living, and should be enriched in knowledge and attitudes and should increasingly take his place as a member of a group rather than needing individual attention. Most of the children will be going into kindergarten at the end of this quarter.

Since some families spend the summer at a summer resort, there may be children who do not attend their own church school during this season. Be sure to give or mail *My Book for Summer* to any child who is absent, with the suggestion that it be used at home. Perhaps the child will attend a church-school group while on vacation. A friendly interest will be shown by teachers who mail *My Picture Card* for the month to children who are to be on vacation. Then, home and church working together, continue to nurture the child religiously during vacation.

There may be new children who are part of your group during all or part of the summer. You may need to order a few extra copies of *My Book for Summer* and *My Picture Card* so that you may give them to such long-term visitors. You may have frequent visitors for a session or two. These visitors should receive *My Picture Card* each Sunday. Recall suggestions in the teacher's helps for October for helping newcomers to feel at home. (See page 98.)

You may need to arrange for one or more additional workers for the summer months, due to increased enrollment, long-term visitors, or to absences of regular workers due to vacation trips. If so, be sure that these extra workers are supplied with the teacher's textbook, pupil's material, and *Child Guidance in Christian Living*. Be sure also that these substitute teachers understand the regular procedures. The children should still wear name tags. The tags will help the new workers to know the name of each girl and boy. If any child receives this book as his first copy, take it to him in his home and talk with his parents about how it is to be used, explaining what your Sunday procedures are and sharing your purposes.

Plans for this quarter include a session on thunderstorms, page 184. This session should be used on a Sunday when a thunderstorm breaks during the session or there has been a thunderstorm on Friday or Saturday. As always nursery plans are flexible—they are for the religious nurture of the children.

Summer supplies including *My Book for Summer* should be ordered early. The letter in the books should be signed by each of the regular teachers before any leave for vacation. Readjustments in sessions will be made according to need as usual. When July has five Sundays, use the suggestions of a Sunday in August for the fifth session. If there are no thunderstorms in July you may decide to skip that session until later. As always, follow the lead and need of the children and plan accordingly.

July

Possible Stories for July (select from these stories in *My Book for Summer*, Part 4): "Picnic Fun," "On the Farm," "Grandmother's Pet Hen," "Watching the Storm."

Possible Songs for July: "New Chicks," "Water," "The Children's Friend," "Friends at Church," "Church Bells."

Possible Pictures for July: "Grandmother's Pet Hen," "When Jesus Was a Little Boy," from *Nursery Class Pictures.* See also, page 180.

Possible Activities for July: Enjoy postcards received from teachers or children. Play picnic. Play thunderstorms with blocks and flashlight. Talk about air-conditioning unit. Play a simple game and finger play. Play in housekeeping center, and with blocks and farm animals. Play delivering milk.

My Picture Card: Select from July, August, September.

DURING THE NEXT TWO MONTHS WEATHER IS LIKELY TO BE HOT AND bright. Workers should do all they can to keep the room for three-year-olds comfortable, eliminating glare as nearly as possible. If electric fans are used, they should be the type that are fastened high on the wall where they are absolutely inaccessible to the children.

If your building is air conditioned it is important that you watch the temperature of the nursery class room and safeguard the children from being chilled.

Provision should be made for cool water to drink. In planning each session, workers should include rest times. This may be a general rest time for all children in longer sessions. In one-hour sessions, protection against fatigue may be secured by careful alternation of times of rest or quiet activity with more active forms of play.

Be sure to include the thunderstorm session this month if it is appropriate to do so. (See page 184.)

Purpose

To provide experiences through which three-year-olds will be helped to a richer enjoyment of family life including summer outings and a possible visit to a farm; to establish more fully a sense of security.

Suggested Bible Study for Teachers

Read through one or more of the Gospels. As you read, mark the references to the outdoors. Note how often the big events in the life of Christ occurred "on a mountain," "on a hillside," "beside the sea," "in a boat." Consider the background of Jesus' friends. As you read the quotations from the teachings of Jesus and the stories he told, mark the verses in which he referred to farmers, shepherds, fishermen, and other people whose lives were largely spent outdoors. Note the disciples who had outdoor occupations.

As you enjoy summer experiences with other adults and with the children of the nursery class, your association should be enriched through such a study as this.

Preparations for July Sessions

Sign pupils' books.

Read suggestions for entire month of July, pages 179 to 186. Read *My Book for Summer*.

Read "Goals and Purposes for the Nursery Class," pages 7-14. Eliminate glare and provide for cool water to drink.

If you have an extended session, ask the mothers to provide bath towels or mats for use during rest periods.

Have ready picture books and magazine pictures of families enjoying picnics, cooking and eating outdoors, hen, rooster and baby chicks, a child talking on telephone, lightning flashes and rain falling. Clip and mount pictures from *My Book for Summer*.

Have ready picture post cards received from teacher and children on vacation.

Provide a small basket or box for playing picnic. Graham crackers, carrot strips, or pieces of apple may be the "picnic lunch." Also two or three hard-boiled eggs and a knife to slice them.

Have ready wooden people and farm animals for dramatic play. Empty milk and egg cartons may also be used.

Have ready two blocks to make the sound of thunder and a small flashlight to make the flash of lightning.

Borrow from a library *Here and Now Story Book* and *Another Here and Now Story Book* by Lucy Sprague Mitchell. In addition to the many excellent stories, you will find them valuable as guides to developing your own skill in living with children, discovering their interests, and developing your own stories.

SUGGESTED PROCEDURE

FIRST SUNDAY

As the children arrive comment on warm weather clothes. As money is put into the offering container, comment that our church uses the money to help people learn about God and Jesus. Sing "Friends at Church" or "Church Bells," page 214.

Most of the children will find activities for themselves now with very little assistance.

Call attention to pictures of families enjoying picnics, cooking and eating outdoors.

Show children any picture post cards received from teachers or children who are traveling. Mention how friendly it is for persons to send a card when on vacation.

Encourage small groups to play picnic or packing a box or basket for an outdoor meal. If it is not practical to go outside to play picnic, small groups may take a walk around the room, each with a teacher. Choose a spot on the floor and play that this is an outdoor picnic. If it is possible to do so, go outdoors under a tree or in the shade of the building to enjoy the picnic.

Serve the picnic lunch of graham crackers, carrot strips or apple quarters. A brief thank-you prayer should be used. While the children are eating, tell the story, "Picnic Fun," *My Book for Summer*. Talk about the good times families have on a picnic.

Play games, pretending that they are part of the picnic fun. The prayer before going indoors, or before returning to play if the picnic was inside, may be, "Thank you, God, for happy times outdoors in summertime. Amen."

Suggest that children enjoy songs and listening to the piano or record player. Use *My Book* records.

Encourage painting with damp, colored chalk on large sheets of paper; building of fences, barns, and farm houses, and play with wooden people and farm animals.

Allow ample time for putting away toys before the parents come and for having a few minutes to look at *My Book for Summer* which will be given out today. Give also, *My Picture Card*, Number 1.

As children are called for, remind them to tell Mother and Daddy about the picnic. Be sure to speak to the parents of visiting children and invite them to come again. (Children who are to be visiting three or more Sundays should be given a copy of *My Book for Summer*.)

SECOND SUNDAY

As the children arrive, express appreciation for our pleasant room where we can work and play.

If your church is air-conditioned and one part of the equipment is in the nursery classroom, there will be great interest in sounds from the unit. In one church, the humming noise of the unit attracted attention. Julian announced, "That's the fan."

"You are right, Julian," said the teacher. "We cannot see it, but we can feel the vibration when we put our hands against the side of the air conditioner." The word vibration was new. So the teacher put her hand against the unit as she said, "I feel the vibration. It shakes." Immediately, each child put his hand against the unit. "I feel the vibration," said Julian. This led naturally to expression of appreciation for a cool room. After this experience, the children went back to their usual activities.

If it is very hot and sunny outdoors, it will be best to spend the entire session indoors. If children play energetically and become warm, have them rest for a while and give them a cool drink of water. Say, "How glad we are for cool, good water to drink." Sing "Water, Water, Water" to the tune, "Church," page 224.

Show pictures of a hen, a rooster, and baby chicks. Sing the scale using the words, "Cluck, cluck, cluck," for the mother hen and "Peep, peep, peep," for the baby chick, and "Cockle-doodle-doo" for the daddy rooster. They may also sing "New Chicks," page 219.

Encourage the children to talk and ask questions. It may surprise you to learn how little they know about chickens. The children may enjoy the story, "Grandmother's Pet Hen," *My Book for Summer*. Pause, then pray, "Dear God, we are glad for hens to give us good eggs to eat. Thank you. Amen." Encourage discussion of the picture.

Have ready two or three hard-boiled eggs. Ask two or three children to close their eyes. Hide the hard-boiled eggs around the room and let these children "find" them. Be sure to hide in places easy to find. Continue the fun as long as small groups are interested.

Serve slices of hard-boiled eggs, perhaps playing picnic again and recalling the picnic play of last session.

In an expanded session there may be an opportunity to play going to the store to buy eggs. Empty egg cartons may be used.

Continue to intersperse times of listening and resting with active play. Just as three or four children can enjoy taking turns in jumping from the overturned rocking boat, or the walking board, so three or four can sit quietly, close their eyes and rest for a few moments, while other activities go on in a different part of the room. Perhaps they may listen to music as they rest.

Sing "Friends at Church," to groups of children who are having a happy time together. Comment, "Dianne, I am going to sing a song about you and Billie because you are friends and you seem to be having such a happy time together." Or, "This song is about Margie and Billie and Michael and Forrest, who have had such a good time hunting eggs together."

Thankfulness for friends means thankfulness for specific friends and should be related to definite, recognized experiences with them if it is to be felt by a three-year-old.

As children leave, you may comment, "We have had a happy time with our friends today." Give *My Picture Card,* Number 2, to each child and suggest that he tell Grandfather (or some other member of the family) about the story.

THIRD SUNDAY

As children arrive, follow the usual procedure. If there are visitors, learn their names and whom they are visiting. Suggest that one of the children go with a teacher to show the visitor the room and to help him find something to do.

Encourage repetition of activities enjoyed already this month, related to picnic fun and the finding of eggs. Continue other activities.

Children will be interested in looking at books showing farm pictures.

If there are large wooden cows at the block center, encourage the building of a farm. Talk about cows giving fresh milk. One or two children may play milkman and deliver the milk to the housekeeping center. This may lead to simple conversation about the milkman who delivers milk. It may also lead to discussion of such milk products as cottage cheese, ice cream, and butter. Suggest that the housekeeper thank the milkman for bringing the milk.

Sing "My Friends," page 219, substituting the word milkman.

If a story is needed, tell "On the Farm," *My Book for Summer.*

Encourage shopping for milk and eggs. Use empty milk and egg cartons. Talk about eating fresh eggs and drinking good milk.

Play "Now I'm Very, Very Small, I'll eat eggs and grow up tall," or "I'll drink milk and grow up tall." (See page 207.)

Play finger game of mother hen and the chicks, *My Book for Summer,* and sing "New Chicks," page 219.

Continue alternation of active and quiet play, noting carefully that no child becomes overheated. Give each child *My Picture Card,* Number 3.

As the children leave, suggest to the parents who call for them that they try to take their children to visit a farm this week to see cows and chickens.

After the Session

Are the children increasing in ability to follow their own interests and to work and play in small groups? If you are to go on vacation, have you talked it over with the nursery class superintendent so that a prepared teacher will substitute for you? It is important that substitute workers know the informal procedures of the nursery class.

FOURTH SUNDAY

As the children come, encourage any who have visited a farm during the week to tell about it. Ask that they tell it so that other children may hear, also.

The plans suggested here are to be used if and when there are thunderstorms, with lightning and showers. Like other similar plans regarding the weather, these will not have meaning for nursery children unless they fit in with their immediate experience. If there was a thunderstorm the last of the week, recall the thunder and lightning.

If there have been no thunderstorms, repeat the activities and use pictures, stories, songs, and prayers suggested in plans for the first three Sundays of this month.

If there is a thunderstorm, you may wish to play "Thunderstorm." Two blocks and a small size flashlight may be used to help the children "enjoy" thunderstorms.

The teacher may demonstrate the use of the blocks and flashlight, then give opportunity for the children to take turns clapping the thunder and flashing the lightning.

The teacher may say, "All the flowers were thirsty. Leaves on the trees were dusty. The grass was dry. The children were hot. *Flash-*

flash went the lightning (flashlight). *Boom, boom* went the thunder (blocks clapped together) and *down* came the rain.

"It gave a drink to the flowers. It made the grass green and fresh. It washed the leaves on the trees. It made the children feel cool. They were glad for the rain.

"Mother said, 'Thank you, God, for the cool rain. Thank you for the noisy thunder and bright lightning that help make us feel cooler. Amen.' "

In one group where this story and activity were used, requests to "tell it again," with various children taking turns with the flashlight and blocks meant that the teacher told the story seventeen times during the session—some children hearing it several times, some only hearing it once or twice.

You may also tell the story, "Watching the Storm," *My Book for Summer.* Ask one or two children to stand near the piano with you and listen as the musician plays some loud, low chords, which sound like the rumble of thunder. A piece of paper, spread on the floor may be tapped to imitate the pitter patter of rain.

Look at and talk about raincoats, rain hats, boots, and umbrellas.

If children mention being afraid of thunder or lightning, talk quietly and pleasantly with them about it. You may have an opportunity to give some wise counsel to parents about dealing with this problem at home. It helps a child to know that you understand and sympathize with his problem. It also helps greatly if his attention is diverted.

In the housekeeping area, you may pretend that you are making cookies or fudge while it storms outside. You may play that children are playing outdoors when a big flash of lightning and the boom, boom of thunder warn that a storm is coming. Call the children to come inside.

While this sort of dramatic play is teacher dominated, such domination is justified if it is helpful in relieving real fears of a child or children. Perhaps only one or two of the children will join in this. It is not important to urge others to do so, especially if you know which children have need of help in this experience.

It is often possible to divert the attention of children in this way so that the dreaded thunderstorm becomes a fascinating game. If it is raining, be sure that the children have an opportunity to watch from the window. They may watch the raindrops splash in the puddles or against other buildings or against the windowpanes. Some of the children may tell of putting on bathing suits and going out to play if there has been rain during the week.

We need to remember that sometimes thunderstorms and tornadoes cause disasters. Such an experience will cause real fear. We can talk about friends helping one another and say thank you to God for friends who help. It is important to avoid any suggestion that will make the child feel, "God sent the storm." It is possible to ask God to help us be brave. It is important to stress the fact that we work with God when we do those things we know are the safe things —not standing at a window or under a tree in thunderstorms, and so on.

The leader will seek to make the thunder showers joyous summer occasions. She will speak of the rain that falls as washing the streets or cooling the air and giving the birds puddles in which to bathe. She may speak of the leaves on the trees being washed clean by the rain just as cool water washes the dust from the children's own faces and hands.

Perhaps some of the children will wish to take dolls to the window as the little girl in the story took her doll. The following prayers are suggested: "Thank you, God, for rain. We are glad the birds like the rain. We like it, too" or "We are glad, dear God, that you care for pets and trees and flowers and for us. Help us to enjoy the bright lightning and the thunder that says 'boom, boom.' "

As the children leave, remind them to tell Mother and Daddy about making the noise of thunder with blocks and flashing the flashlight for lightning. Give each *My Picture Card*, Number 4.

If July has five Sundays, see page 195.

To Think About

Have I used opportunities as they arose, to offer a brief prayer with the two or three children with whom I have been working? Has each child in the group been in such a small informal group at a time when a prayer was offered?

How may I make greater use of songs, with or without the piano or record player, as the children play?

How have I planned new ideas to use during the summer months? Am I using these plans? Reread goals for the nursery class, page 9. How am I working toward attaining these goals?

August

POSSIBLE MATERIALS AND ACTIVITIES

Possible Stories for August (select from these stories in *My Book for Summer,* Part 4): "When Jesus Was a Little Boy," "The Tricycle Airplane," "Good Water," "Surprises," "Down by the Ocean."

Possible Songs for August: "Little Baby Jesus," "Friends," "Taking Turns," "Water," "Friends at Church."

Possible Pictures for August: "When Jesus Was a Little Boy," "Down by the Ocean," from *Nursery Class Pictures.* See also, page 189.

Possible Activities for August: Look at objects brought back from vacations. Listen to a seashell. Play birds splashing in water. Place a pan of water for a birdbath. Play thunder and lightning game. Play fishing. Examine small objects through magnifying glass. Take turns on tricycle to play "pilot" on plane. Skip to music and listen to music. Use musical instruments.

My Picture Card: Select from July, August, September.

SUMMER PROBLEMS WILL CONTINUE DURING AUGUST. ATTENDANCE may fluctuate and the membership of the group will change as children go on and come from vacations. Although the group may be small, meeting with them will be worthwhile for the leaders can help the children to develop a sense of appreciation for and joy in vacation experiences and continue to guide their social life in the church.

During August there are likely to be thunderstorms. Occasionally such a thunderstorm may occur during the church-school session. Some of the children will need to be reassured. There may be the opportunities to enjoy the flash of lightning or to play making the noise of thunder with blocks. This play helps overcome a fear that many adults have not entirely outgrown.

During the hot weather nursery children are likely to suffer from digestive disorders and attendant physical upsets. These may cause and be caused by emotional disturbances so that, frequently, the leader should provide opportunities for the children to play alone and so to avoid any conflicts that may arise in group play.

It is also necessary for the leader to watch carefully as the children get drinks of water. They should not drink too much at one time nor should the water be too cold.

The older children in the group will have passed their fourth birthday during the year. Some of these children will have learned to skip. Others, past four, will still skip by hopping on one foot. For variation, the nursery leader may borrow from the kindergarten the record album, *Sing, O Sing*.[1] On the "B" side of record 504, she will find "Skip in C" and "Fun in a Swing." Both of these are activities that fours may enjoy. For "Skip in C" the children will skip to the music. "Fun in a Swing" may be played as two children face one another, join hands, and swing back and forth keeping time with the music.

Record 501 may be borrowed for use with the story, "When Jesus Was a Little Boy," as suggested in Session 1, page 189.

Purpose

To help three-year-olds to begin to realize that Jesus grew as they grow; to encourage the children in sharing and taking turns; to provide opportunities for enjoying some wonders in God's world and to express appreciation for water as a part of God's wonderful plan.

Suggested Bible Study for Teachers

Classic examples of beautiful prose and poetry are to be found in the Bible. Many of these deal with the gentleness, power, and awesomeness of the elements. Psalms 23, 104, 107, many other Psalms, Job 36 and 37 and other passages from Job, as well as some of the beautiful passages from the Prophets, such as the fifty-fifth chapter of Isaiah are examples. Read these listed above and search for others.

Another beautiful poem is the Song of Mary and the angels' song. Read again Luke 1:46-56; 2:8-14.

Preparations for August Sessions

Continue to keep the room as cool and comfortable as possible. Provide cool drinking water and paper cups.

Set up materials and equipment which will encourage children to enjoy quiet as well as active play. Include toy airplane.

Provide an aquarium with fish.

Provide a few simple rhythm band type instruments, such as triangles, drums, tambourines, rhythm sticks, marimba.

Secure books of airplanes, automobiles, and trains.

---

[1] *Sing, O Sing*. Price, $2.95. May be secured from The Methodist Publishing House serving you.

Have ready pictures of Jesus as a baby, as a little boy, and as a man.

Mount pictures of children enjoying water play in the bathtub, and at the seashore, also pictures of birds bathing. These may be placed on the tackboard, made into a picture book or a picture box, and used on the book table. Some of these pictures may be clipped from *My Book for Summer* or from *My Picture Card*.

Have available a reading glass or magnifying glass.

Secure blades of grass, a small stone, a few grains of sand.

Have ready a conch shell.

Provide a small basin for a birdbath.

Have ready a small size flashlight.

Have ready paper or envelopes for playing "mail" delivered by plane.

Borrow a tricycle for dramatic plane play.

Secure records and have record player ready.

SUGGESTED PROCEDURE

FIRST SUNDAY

If some children have been away for a trip, encourage them to tell about it. If teachers and parents have brought interesting outdoor items from mountains, seashore, or the country, display these and call attention to them.

Tiny cones, and very large ones are interesting. If possible, get some of the winged seeds from them to show to the children.

In the housekeeping center, play getting ready for company. Dress the dolls. Prepare an imaginary meal.

Talk together about the way the children help at home—drying dishes, making beds, coming quickly when Mother or Father or someone else calls.

Discuss what they like to play. Do you play with a ball? Sit in a circle with five or six children. Let them spread their feet apart. Play rolling a big ball from child to child, calling the name of the child to whom the ball is to be rolled.

Do you like to play with blocks? If block play seems interesting, encourage it.

Do you like to hear Mother or Daddy or someone tell stories?

Tell the story, "When Jesus Was a Little Boy," *My Book for Summer*.

Look at the picture, "When Jesus Was a Little Boy." What is Jesus doing? Jesus had baby brothers and sisters. Perhaps the baby is asleep while little boy Jesus and Mother Mary are talking.

Suggest that the children listen to some records. "Away in a Manger," "Silent Night," "Little Baby Jesus," or some other favorite Christmas carol may recall when Jesus was a baby.

In the kindergarten record album, *Sing, O Sing*, record 501, Side A has the carol, "Away in a Manger," and the songs, "The Boy Jesus" and "The Children's Friend." If these have been borrowed from the kindergarten they may be enjoyed now.

After listening to the records, suggest that the children look at books, or take a nap with the dolls. Dolls may take their naps on a bed made of a big block, while the children who have been playing in the housekeeping center spread towels or mats on the floor for a rest. Either dolls or a child may "nap" in the doll bed.

Offer suggestions when they seem needed, but do not hesitate to sit down quietly and look on when children are happily engaged in their own interesting activities. By this time of year the children should be well acquainted and able to enjoy finding their own activities.

As the children put away toys and blocks, the pianist may play several of the songs used during the year. Some children may sing as they work. Some may gather around the piano to sing.

Some children will be interested in using the musical instruments, such as tambourines, marimba, triangles, sticks to tap, and drums. They may wish to use these in marching in the parade. The musician or the record player may provide marching music. When this has been enjoyed for a while, you may suggest that the children sit on the floor to rest. Sing "Friends at Church," page 214.

If there is interest in doing so, play "Getting Ready for Nursery Class," "Teeter-Totter," or "Now I'm Very, Very Small," until the parents come for the children.

Give *My Picture Card*, Number 5, to each child. Remind the children to tell the story to Mother, Father, Grandmother—or whoever comes for them.

SECOND SUNDAY

As the children arrive, suggest that money be placed in the offering basket as usual. You may mention something for which it is used, such as paying for the copies of *My Book for Summer*.

Give children who have taken a trip an opportunity to talk about it. If you will keep in touch with parents and ask that they tell you something of their trips with their children, you will be able to ask questions and make comments in such a way as to encourage children to tell you about their trips.

Perhaps there will be interest in singing well-known favorite songs with piano or record player accompaniment or without music. Especially appropriate songs would be "God's Care," page 224, "Jesus Saw the Flowers," page 225, or "Taking Turns," page 221.

Doll play may be encouraged again this Sunday. If it is possible to have a new airplane, or a fleet of small ones, they may be on the toy shelf or in a place where the children can find them readily. Encourage the children to play with, talk about, and take turns using the planes. Discuss how planes are used for carrying mail and passengers. There may be conversation about mail being carried to Grandmother or to some other relative or to a friend. Small bits of paper or the envelopes that the leader brought may be put in the plane while the children pretend that it is flying and then that it lands. The mail may be taken out and handed out as letters that came from the mail plane.

It is likely that many will have stories to tell about taking a trip by plane or going to the airport to meet someone. Let them discuss the servicing of the plane if interest warrants. Using the toy planes will probably have special interest, also building planes with blocks, putting in the gas, loading baggage, and so on.

If a story is used, "The Tricycle Airplane" from *My Book for Summer,* is suggested. Perhaps just conversation about planes and what fun it is to travel in a plane may be used instead of a story. It is likely that all of the children will be interested in talking about the way planes fly over the houses and higher than the church and how they sparkle in the sunlight. Some of the children may mention seeing the red and green lights on the plane as it flies by night.

This session should provide an opportunity for establishing a sense of security. The leader will seek to safeguard the children from any experiences that might lead to fear of planes. The rocking boat or a plane built of large blocks may be used for playing airplane.

If the story is used, you may wish to borrow a tricycle for use indoors or out as the children play airplane or automobile, and take turns being the "pilot" of the airplane or the driver of the automobile. The air mail letters or the special letter from Grandmother or Aunt Maggie may be delivered.

Conversation may be about careful drivers of automobiles and tricycles and careful pilots of airplane tricycles.

If there is time and the children are interested in skipping or swinging to music, record 504 B of the album, *Sing, O Sing,* may be borrowed from the kindergarten and used again this session.

As the children leave, give each *My Picture Card,* Number 6, and remind each to be a careful driver or pilot.

THIRD SUNDAY

Be sure to welcome children who have been on vacation or have been absent for any other reason. Share any cards that have been received.

Encourage the children to find their favorite activity. Some may wish to work puzzles. Some may enjoy the books while others engage in play at the block or the housekeeping center.

One teacher may guide two or three children at a time to look at and talk about the pictures showing water activities. She will also guide the small groups to the aquarium.

Some of the children may notice the pictures of children taking a bath or of birds bathing. Conversation will start normally from this interest. Otherwise, the leader will call attention to the pictures after the children have played informally. Perhaps two or three children may look at the pictures with the leader at one time. Speak of the joy of playing in the water. Some of the children may tell of the fun they have in a tub of water in the back yard, or they may report putting on sunsuits or bathing suits and splashing in the puddles after a shower or playing under the spray from the lawn hose. Still others may wish to tell about birds they have watched bathing in the puddles. If this is reported, the child who tells it may be willing to show how the bird fluffs out his wings. The leader may play softly and the older children may be interested to fly around hunting an imaginary puddle and pretending to fluff their wings and splash around as the birds do when they take their baths.

The leader will speak of how much the birds need water for bathing and drinking. If there has been rain during the past week, the children may recall this and a prayer may be appropriate. "Thank you, God, for rain. We are glad the birds like rain. We like it, too" or "Thank you, God, for the birds. We like to help take care of them."

Conversation will have developed ideas of helping to care for the birds. The children may recall that earlier in the year they placed bits of string for nests. A few may remember how they scattered crumbs during the cold weather. The leader may say, "Now the birds have finished with their nests. They can find seeds to eat also. But we may place pans of water so that they may take a bath." If there is a bird-bath on the church lawn, call attention to it.

Sing "God's Care," page 224.

If there is a space where a basin might serve as a birdbath, the leader may have a small basin ready and the children may decide where to place it. Then there will be the fun of filling the new birdbath with water. If possible, such a birdbath should be placed so that it can be seen from the nursery class windows. Then the children may watch frequently for the birds and the birds will not be frightened away by having the children too close to them.

A small aquarium with two or three goldfish will prove interesting. It provides another evidence of God's plan. We live in homes with Mother and Daddy. Baby birds live in nests. But fish live in water. Water is the home for the fish. We have water to cool us off, water to drink, water to wash the dusty flowers and trees, water for a bath, water for a home for the fish.

There will probably be several opportunities for a thank-you prayer in this session.

There may be no time for a story on this Sunday, or the discussion of birds having a bath or the fun of playing in the water may lead to the story, "Good Water," *My Book for Summer*. "Thank you, God, for good water. We like to drink water. We like to play in water. We like to have a bath" might be an appropriate prayer.

Provide cool drinking water.

Sing "Water," tune, "Church," page 224.

The children may play "Taking a bath," using the tune, "Mulberry Bush." They may sing,

> "This is the way I wash my face
> This is the way I wash my hands,
> This is the way I wash my feet,
> This is the way I rub with the towel"

and so on. They may also enjoy singing "All of Me," page 226.

As the children leave, give them *My Picture Card*, Number 7, and ask the parents to provide opportunities for water play during the week and to use the prayer on the card for today.

FOURTH SUNDAY

As usual, greet the children, encourage them to put their offering in the container and discuss the fun that they are having this summer. Have they been on a picnic, had visitors, gone away? If they have been away, did they travel by car, bus, train, or plane?

In the housekeeping center, encourage usual play. Perhaps it will be possible to play thunderstorm and encourage the children to care for their babies.

Two children may be responsible for thunder and lightning.

Two or three others may tell the dolls how the lightning flashes, and the thunder goes *boom, boom* and the rain comes down.

The aquarium may be another center of interest for two or three children. Let them look at the fish through the sides of the aquarium and also look down into the top of aquarium. The children may help put fish food in the water. This is strictly a teacher supervised activity lest the fish be overfed.

On one table have a reading or magnifying glass, some small flowers, as clover, baby's breath, dandelion, sweet alyssum, or others. Have also a few blades of grass, a small stone, and a few grains of sand. A teacher will be at this table, ready to guide.

Encourage the children to use the glass and to talk about what they see. The teacher who is guiding these observations will be careful to follow the lead of the children and only to offer suggestions when the boys and girls do not know how to use the glass or how to look at objects through it.

"This is a glass that makes everything look larger. Look through the glass at this little blade of grass." Taking turns looking through the glass will require real patience.

If a story is used this session, "Surprises," *My Book for Summer*, may be told over and over again at the table to each of the small groups of two or three children who may be using the glass.

A suggested prayer is, "We are so glad to see some little things through the glass. Thank you, God, for little things in our world. Amen."

The game, "Getting Ready for Nursery Class," page 208, may be played, or the children may again enjoy using "Skip in C," or "Fun in a Swing." (See page 188.)

Some of the children may enjoy listening to music on the record player, or at the piano. Or there may be time for reuse of songs enjoyed during the year as three or four children sing around the piano.

The leader needs constantly to remember that informal procedures in the nursery class will provide for the entire group to be engaged in following interests in many different interest groups. One to three or four children may be block building or housekeeping, or at the book table or aquarium. Some may be using the magnifying glass or listening to the record player. Still a few others may be at the piano.

As the children leave, remind them to tell Mother and Daddy (or Grandmother) about the wonderful glass that made everything look big. Give each child *My Picture Card,* Number 8, and remind him, "See you next Sunday."

FIFTH SUNDAY

Since there are thirteen Sundays in each quarter, you will have a fifth Sunday during one month of each quarter. If this fifth Sunday is not in August, these plans may be used on the fifth Sunday in July or the first Sunday in September.

As the children arrive, guide them to find interesting things to do.

Repeat any activities, stories, songs, prayers, or games which have been enjoyed already during the month.

If you have a birdbath outside your window, keep it filled with water and watch for birds getting water to drink or taking baths. (See page 193.)

If some children are going on or returning from a vacation trip, encourage them to tell about it. Thank any who sent cards. Speak of how nice it is to have friends remember to send cards when away from home.

In parts of the country where the children will have been likely to have enjoyed a day or longer at the shore, they will enter more fully into conversation about the fun of digging in the sand, playing in the water, and watching the waves roll in. Some may have collected pretty stones and shells to share with the group.

Enjoy pictures of children playing at the seashore, looking at shells, building sand castles, and so on.

A sea shell will afford much interest. You may speak of its beauty. "This is a conch shell. It is lovely inside. It is shining and pink. It was once the home of a little creature known as a conch. (Three-year-olds like that word.) When a big wave washed it up on the sandy seashore, the conch moved out. Even though the shell is now a long way from the sea, you can still hear a sound when you hold it close to your ear.

This sound will make you think of the sea." Pray, "Thank you, God, for big waves. We like to hear wave sounds in a shell. Amen." The foregoing conversation and prayer may be adapted to whatever is shared with the group—small shells, cones, snails, pretty rocks and stones, driftwood.

Talk about the fun of playing in the waves and digging in the sand. Some children may mention boats. Perhaps you can play boats, using the rocking boat. If you have no rocking boat, build the outline of a boat with blocks. Let the children sit "inside" the boat. A long block may be used as a fishing rod. Or chairs may be used as a boat and the children can play that they are fishing over the chair backs.

Sing "Water," or "Ocean," "River," "Lake," to the tune "Church," page 224, using whichever body of water may be known to your group.

If a story is told, "Down by the Ocean" from *My Book for Summer,* will be used. Perhaps this story can be told on a beach rug or large bath towel. The teacher and two or three children may sit on the towel, pretending that they are watching the ocean as the teacher tells the story. If this plan is used, the story will need to be told several times until all who wish to hear it have a turn.

Enjoy together the large picture, "Down by the Ocean."

Encourage conversation about watching the waves or watching the sunset (on lake or river for children who have not seen the ocean).

The record, "Fun in a Swing," may be used as the children play that they are in a boat, going up and down on the waves. (See page 188.)

There may be interest in listening to music again this session.

Each child will receive *My Picture Card*, Number 9, as he leaves.

Ask Yourself

Have I shown patience as a Christian leader entrusted by my church to nurture the religious growth of young children?

September

POSSIBLE MATERIALS AND ACTIVITIES

Possible Stories for September (select from these stories
in *My Book for Summer*, Part 4): "Happy Birthday,"
"Bedtime," "Hello, Aunt Betty," "Big Enough to Help."

Possible Songs for September: "Friends at Church,"
"Friends," "The Children's Friend," "Taking Turns,"
"Growing," "All of Me."

Possible Pictures for September: "Thank You, God,"
"When Jesus Was a Little Boy," "Down by the Ocean,"
from *Nursery Class Pictures.* See also page 200.

Possible Activities for September: Continue to enjoy
post cards and objects brought back from vacations. Play
a game of growing up. Measure children's height. Play
making a birthday cake. Play outdoors. Visit a fall
garden. Enjoy listening to music and playing rhythm
instruments. Enjoy toy telephone. Visit from the kindergarten teacher.

My Picture Card: Select from July, August, September.

THERE WILL BE A CONTINUATION OF IRREGULAR ATTENDANCE
during September, but the greatest problem for most nursery workers
is that of promotion. The irregular attendance of the children and the
program that is likely to be somewhat disrupted in both the two- and
three-year-old nursery classes usually make it advisable not to risk
the emotional strain of having children promoted before September.

The leader will read suggestions for promotion on page 85,
and will decide on the procedures for her own group. Suggestions are
included this month for possible procedures that look toward the
promotion from nursery class to kindergarten.

The leader will seek to provide a natural, normal, and calm plan
of promotion. The leader of the four-year-old group will visit the
nursery class on the third Sunday. (You may decide to invite her
for two sessions—the second and third Sundays.)

All exploitation of the children will be avoided. That is, there will
be no "promotion exercises" in which the nursery children appear
with older groups or before the school assembly. The leader will
seek to help the children who are not to be promoted to realize that
they are growing bigger, that they are to continue to be the helpers

in the nursery class after the older girls and boys have gone to the kindergarten. The leader may also emphasize that the three-year-olds are big enough to help at home. They may put away their own toys. They may come quickly when Mother and Daddy call them. In this way she will guard against making promotion such a desired goal that discontent would be felt by those who are not being promoted.

It might be well this month to check the development of each child in terms of the goals for Christian education for nursery children, as listed on pages 9 through 12. Ask yourself and one another for evidences of happiness in belonging to the church group, enjoyment of fellowship with adults and children at church school, and recognition of himself as a part of the church by each child.

Have the children learned about God's care because of experiences during this year? Have they learned to know the name of Jesus and to think of him as a baby whose family loved and cared for him and whose birthday we celebrate at Christmas? Do they think of Jesus the boy, growing up in a family? Do they know Jesus as a special person who was a friend of children? Do they think of the Bible as a special book that tells about God and Jesus?

Have they learned some happy ways of living with others because they have come to nursery class? Do they share and take turns more readily than when they entered nursery class?

Such intangibles cannot be measured easily, but as you come to the close of this year and look forward to another, it would be well to consider them as you think of each child who is to leave your group and enter the kindergarten.

Purpose

To help nursery children begin to recognize growth and development as part of God's plan.

Suggested Bible Study for Teachers

Read Matthew 22:36-40.

In this command that we shall love God with all of our faculties and our neighbor as ourselves, Jesus put into words what might well be called a philosophy of Christian education. If we who are teachers of children truly love God with our intelligence, our emotions, and our physical energies, we will find that we are able to help little children come to know and love him, too. As for loving our neighbor as ourselves, we might do well to ask, "Who is my neighbor?" as did the people in the situation described here in the Bible. It would be wise also to look at the way in which we love ourselves. We cannot love others until we have a sense of recognition of self. Jesus certainly did not mean pampering, flattering love for oneself. Nor did he mean such "love" for one's neighbor. Whether it be at the level of experience of the child who is three or four years old, or at a more mature level, there are certain essential elements in love which will result in human relationships worthy of being called Christian. The same evidences of Christian living should not be expected of the four-year-old as of his fifty-year-old grandparents. But the basic foundation for such Christian living should be laid. You may think through and determine what you believe these basic foundations to be.

As you read the Gospels, note what Jesus taught concerning one's attitude toward and treatment of others. Summarize these. Some of these teachings will be:

Respect for oneself and others as persons.

Self-forgetfulness so that one's neighbor may have all the good things one would desire for himself.

Forgiveness of others.

This thoughtful examination of one's own philosophy of Christian education as measured by the teachings of Jesus will become more meaningful to each teacher who uses it.

Preparations for September Sessions

Arrange room with centers for activities as before.

Provide a few simple, rhythm band-type instruments, such as triangles, drums, tambourines, rhythm sticks, marimba.

Have one or two toy telephones.

The leader may make a telephone taking two large spools and tying a cord to each. The children can hold the spool so that they will play that they are talking in one end while listening in the other end. Or a telephone may be made from two small tin cans that have been opened so that there are no sharp or rough edges. A string may be attached to each can through a small hole pierced in the bottom. This makes an admirable telephone either painted or left unpainted. At least four feet of string should extend between the spools or cans. It would be well to provide more than one telephone.

Continue to have growing plants and early fall flowers in the room.

Clip from magazines pictures showing children celebrating birthdays, assuming responsibility at home, and playing with friends.

Provide for a variety of activities, some to interest older children almost ready for kindergarten and some for the three-year-olds who have been in the nursery class for only a few weeks. Provide a yardstick and large sheet of wrapping paper to measure the children's height.

Prepare a list of names, addresses, and any other information that should be provided for the kindergarten leader. Frequently such a list includes special items such as "Enjoys puzzles. Has new baby sister," or "Has made real social adjustments this year."

You may be asked to give a duplicate list of the names of children to the church office for the records.

Many nursery class teachers write a letter to the parents of each child who is to be promoted. This letter explains reasons for keeping promotion a quiet time. It mentions the name of the kindergarten teachers. A paragraph regarding any evidences of growth on the part of their child is appreciated by parents.

SUGGESTED PROCEDURE

FIRST SUNDAY

Children who are returning after a summer away from home may need help in readjusting to the group. Some will have grown larger, acquired suntans or otherwise changed in appearance.

As children who have been absent come in, if they have sent cards, take them over and show them the cards that have been received. Tell them how much you appreciated and enjoyed the card. Since an adult must write and mail any card from a three-year-old, do not be surprised if the child who sent the greeting does not appear to know anything about it. At the time it was sent, it probably had meaning for him, but such things are quickly forgotten at three.

The picture, "Down by the Ocean," may stimulate reports of vacations.

As the children follow their own interests, the pianist may play the songs used throughout the year. Any of the children who are interested in singing will probably go to the piano and sing with her. Some may wish just to sit and listen. Others probably will enjoy hearing the music as they are busy at the various interest centers.

Some may sing with the music as they work puzzles, build with blocks, or play in the housekeeping center.

Spend some time playing outdoors if possible.

Encourage children to put away toys after they have been used. Play some of the games enjoyed during the year. (See pages 207 to 209.) Mention by name some of the children who are four years old and some who are three years old. Comment that all of us are growing and can do things for ourselves which we could not do before. You may make a game of this by asking children to tell some things they can do and singing about it to the tune, "Here We Go Round the Mulberry Bush."

Three- and four-year-olds do not volunteer much information in response to a group question, so you may have to be more definite. For instance, "Mary, can you button your own shoes? Tommy, can you put your own tricycle in the garage? Sue Ellen, do you bring the milk in from the front step?" This may lead to conversation about home responsibilities and having grown big enough to help at home. Lead in a prayer, "Thank you, God, for girls and boys who are big enough to help at home. Amen."

Show the picture, "When Jesus Was a Little Boy." Talk about Jesus growing up. Tell the story, "Happy Birthday," *My Book for Summer.*

While emphasis on growing big is part of the preparation for Promotion Day, the activities relating to celebration of a birthday may be used at any time during the year when a child has a birthday. Many teachers have commented that not only does the child whose birthday is actually being celebrated wish to talk of his age, or be sung to, but that often others do, too. A record should be kept so that you may know whose birthday comes at each time of year. But, when playing birthday dinner or birthday party, you may repeat the activity for any child who wishes. You may wish to say, "Certainly we'll sing for your birthday. It comes in January (or May or whenever it does come) and you were four years old."

Provide a measuring stick and measure the children, marking their height on a large piece of paper fastened to the wall. Write the name beside the mark of each child measured. Comment on how tall each of them is growing, but do not compare one with another. Rejoice that we are all growing. The number of inches is not meaningful to three-year-olds. They enjoy feeling "big." Measuring adds to this enjoyment.

If there is a birthday, you may wish to promote cake making, talking about it, and playing birthday party in the housekeeping center. You may have a birthday song you like to sing, or children may request the perennial "Happy Birthday to You." Another song appropriate for birthday celebration is "All of Me," page 226.

There will never be an artificial birthday cake or lighted candles in the nursery class.

As children leave, say "I am glad that you are big enough to (mention any help the child has said he does at home). Give each *My Picture Card*, Number 10.

SECOND SUNDAY

There may be some children returning from vacation again this week. Proceed as on other Sundays, greeting each child, expressing appreciation for any card received and pleasure that the child is back again. Encourage reports of the vacation fun.

Encourage usual play and sharing experiences.

In groups of two and three lead the children around the room to see the pictures of children sleeping, getting ready for bed, and so on.

Call attention to pictures showing nighttime experiences, such as children getting ready for bed, saying prayers, and sleeping. Talk of how nice it is to go to bed and go to sleep at the end of a happy day. Tell "Bedtime," *My Book for Summer*. Show picture, "Thank You, God."

Give the children an opportunity to tell you how they get ready for bed, who helps them, if they have stories or prayers, if they sleep alone or with someone. Sing "Sleep," to the tune, "Church," page 224.

In the housekeeping center, encourage play of night time, of putting babies to bed, reading stories, singing lullabies, and praying.

If any parent has shared with you information that a child in your group is afraid of the dark, or fussy about leaving the family at bedtime, you may be able to suggest ideas about the dolls which may be helpful to the child or children involved. Be careful in doing this that you do not suggest unfortunate ways of behaving. You may grow a little weary of always talking and telling stories about sweet, good, happy children, but it is wise to hold up a pattern worthy of imitation and avoid making the undesirable attractive.

Conversation may include the fact that Stevie is a big four-year-old boy but he goes to bed at eight o'clock so he will continue to grow strong. Stevie's big sister Becky stays up a little later than Stevie. When Stevie is ten years old, he will be able to stay up a little later, too.

Enjoy games in small groups. "Getting Ready for Bed" may be sung to the tune of "Mulberry Bush" as the children sing,

> "This is the way I put away my toys,"
> "This is the way I take off my shoes,"
> "This is the way I brush my teeth,"

and so on, mentioning various activities.

Again this Sunday some children may be interested in using the musical instruments, such as tambourines, triangle, and sticks to tap. Others may request the record player. Some will enjoy the skipping or swinging games of the record album, *Sing, O Sing*.

Some may wish to gather near the piano to sing until parents come. Others may sing as they complete puzzles, put away blocks and toys, and so on. Appropriate songs are "All of Me," page 226, "Taking Turns," page 221, and "Growing," page 226.

As the children leave, give each *My Picture Card*, Number 11, and remind them to ask Mother or Daddy to read them the bedtime story.

THIRD SUNDAY

As the children come greet them and comment again to each about age, size, and that soon he will go to the kindergarten or be one of the biggest children in the nursery class.

Encourage the children to look at the pictures of children or adults talking on telephones.

Toy telephones in the housekeeping center may have aroused interest. Telephone conversations between children and a teacher may be guided into invitations to come for dinner.

Talk together about times the children answer the telephone. "Does Grandmother ever call you, Helen?" "Does Daddy call Mother during the day or when he is away from home?" "Does Mother ever let you talk to a friend on the telephone?"

Such conversation may lead to telling the story, "Hello, Aunt Betty," found in *My Book for Summer*.

Be very careful to protect the rights of the youngest children in the group and to provide them with interesting activities which they are capable of carrying through. Do not attempt to push them into activities planned for the older children. Some of these younger children may be interested in playing telephone. But others will have no interest in this dramatic play.

If you have the toy telephones, or spool telephone, a teacher may start playing with the children until interest is aroused. The children themselves should be encouraged to dial the numbers and use the phone for conversation. After dramatic play, you may wish to repeat the story substituting other names for "Aunt Betty."

The younger children will still be interested in playing alone. Encourage their individual play, inviting one or two others into the play as opportunity arises but not forcing co-operative group participation.

The interest should continue in puzzles, in hearing the records on the record player, listening to the piano, and singing familiar songs used throughout the year.

It may be possible to play outdoors or to visit a garden to enjoy fall flowers. If you cannot do this, provide for some active indoor play, such as skipping, marching, and swinging again this Sunday. Once again you may wish to borrow the album, *Sing, O Sing,* from the kindergarten. It is well to use these records and the skipping and singing games during this month as they will be used in kindergarten and the use this last month in nursery class may serve to help the children feel at home in kindergarten.

Suggest that children look at books, listen to stories, work puzzles, draw, or play with floor toys or blocks or with housekeeping toys.

The leading teacher of the four-year-old kindergarten should come into your room for this session. Take her from group to group. Introduce her to each child very informally. Tell her who will be promoted next Sunday and who will stay to be your biggest children. Allow her to move about at will, observing the children and getting acquainted. Special interests may be mentioned, as "Barton is an excellent worker of puzzles," or "Nancy is a good skipper when we skip to music," or "Keith helps us sing," or "Lisa is always ready to help other girls and boys."

In those churches where an outdoor playground is available and the children are accustomed to play with slides, ladders, big building material, and rolling toys, there will be many opportunities to comment on the growth and development of individual children.

As usual, encourage the children to pick up and put away toys before going home. As they go home tell them they will come to this room next Sunday and stay until time to go to the kindergarten. Be sure that families fully understand that the basis of promotion is age. The child will be promoted to the four-year-old kindergarten two years before his entrance into the first grade of public school.

Give each child *My Picture Card,* Number 12.

FOURTH SUNDAY

As the children come, greet them, receive their offering, and suggest activities. Do not make the mistake of just waiting until time for promotion. Carry on the usual activities with housekeeping, blocks, puzzles, books, and so on. Let those who wish gather at the piano to sing.

Mention to each child who will be promoted that he will soon go into the kindergarten. Mention the name of a teacher he will know there. Tell him who some of the others are who will go into the kindergarten with him. Tell each child who will continue to be in the nursery class that soon he or she will be one of the biggest children in the class. Mention that you are counting on him to help you teach the new children how to act in nursery class.

Do not express regret or sorrow that children are leaving you. Promote happy use of play equipment, books, and puzzles until the kindergarten teacher comes to tell you that it is time for the children who are to be promoted to go into the room for four-year-olds. This will depend upon the time that the four-year-olds are promoted to the five-year-old kindergarten. Move quietly from child to child, telling him that it is time now for him to go to kindergarten.

As each group is ready to go to the new room pause for a brief prayer, "Thank you, God, for girls and boys big enough to go to kindergarten. We have had happy times together in nursery class. Help us, as we grow bigger and stronger to be able to help others. Amen."

Sing "Friends at Church," page 214, "Taking Turns," page 221, or "Friends," to the tune "Church," page 224.

One of the teachers will go with each small group of children. If a child suddenly decides he does not want to go, or is afraid, do not insist. You may say, "You are old enough and big enough for the kindergarten and you may go when you are ready." Usually, such a child will go the next Sunday. A few will hold out for several weeks. Some children are not ready although they may have reached the required age.

Be sure to have some interesting suggestion with which to occupy the children who are not promoted. Make them feel important, and keep them busy. Tell the story, "Big Enough to Help," *My Book for Summer*. They may enjoy using the musical instruments. It may be wise to go outside and play in the playground, or if there is no playground to take a walk.

As soon as the four-year-olds are promoted, the children who are being promoted from the two-year-old nursery group will be brought in. Take a walk around the room with these younger children, carrying on a conversation in a calm manner. "This is where we play house," "This is our slide." "Here is where we build with blocks," "At this table we work puzzles," and so on.

When the parents of this new group call for their children, tell them you look forward to a year of enjoyment as you share their child's growth. You may be surprised at the way the older three-year-olds blossom out with the four-year-olds no longer overshadowing them.

Sing "Growing," page 226, and give each *My Picture Card*, Number 13.

To Think About and Do

Look over the list of names of the children who have been promoted to the kindergarten. On a sheet of paper, write down ways in which each child has, you believe, developed.

How have you grown as a nursery class teacher? Reread "The Nursery Class Teacher," pages 32-37, and list two ways in which you will seek to improve next year.

Games

The "Get-Acquainted" Game

An excellent way of getting acquainted and of helping the children to learn one another's names is for the leader to sit on the rug with three or four of the children and ask, "Can you find Mary's ear?" One of the children will be sure to touch Mary's ear. This will be continued with, "Can you find Paul's foot; Bob's hand; Betty's nose?" and so on.

Ball Rolling

Bright-colored balls are always favorites with the children. There may be several variations of rolling the ball. It may be rolled from the leader to a child, back to the leader and to another child, to develop the idea of taking turns, or several children may sit on the floor with legs extended and roll the ball from one to another, each one calling the name of the child to whom the ball is to be rolled. This is another excellent way of getting acquainted, or there may be just the rolling back and forth between two children. The greatest value in this is that of drawing out the shy or bashful child who may be willing to co-operate with one child but is not ready to enter the group.

Leaves Are Falling

While singing the words of the song (page 215), the children twirl around and fall to the floor.

Now I'm Very, Very Small

Three or four children join hands with a leader to form a circle. They stoop on the floor to be small, then stretch up, extending arms above heads to be tall, as they sing,

> Sometimes I'm very, very small
> Sometimes I'm very, very tall.
> Sometimes small,
> Sometimes tall,
> See what I am now.

Ring Rosy

"Ring Rosy" is played in various ways in different sections of the country. Among the simplest versions is this one: A teacher takes one or two children by the hand making a circle. She sings as they go around. If the musician will sing and play, it is helpful. As she sings the words, "Ring around a rosy, pockets full of posy," they move about. As she sings, "Upstairs, downstairs, one, two, three," they stretch their arms up, stoop down, then sit down on the floor. If other children seem to wish it, they may be included in the circle for a repetition of the game. If the group grows large, another teacher may join in. After playing a few moments, the leader may suggest that the group sit still on the floor to rest. She may sing, or the pianist may play quiet music. Or, she may offer a prayer, such as, "Thank you, God, for happy times with my friends at home and at church school."

THE SNOWMAN

This game is sung to the words of "The Snowman," page 217. The children stand with arms extended or over head as they start to sing. Gradually they melt away until they are lying flat on the rug by the time they reach the last words, "see him go."

Frequently it is possible to plan this game just before rest period, and the last time the children melt they may remain lying as they listen to quiet music for a few minutes.

FOLLOW THE LEADER

This is one of the very simple games which may be played in the nursery class. It is great fun to follow some person around the room, behind the piano, winding past chairs, up and down the slide, or around in circles. Frequently, the children will initiate and play the game without giving it any name. Three or four of them may start off after someone who happens to be the leader of that particular group. It is great fun when there is a small limited outdoor space where steps are available so that the children may run up one step and jump down and then around in a circle. Encourage initiative in playing the game. Care must be taken to avoid running and pushing or having the game deteriorate into rough and tumble.

TEETER-TOTTER

With arms extended the children bend to right and left, to represent a teeter-totter, as the words of the song on page 220 are sung.

GETTING READY FOR NURSERY CLASS

This game is a variation of an old favorite. It may be sung to the tune of "Here We Go Round the Mulberry Bush." The children will suggest different ways that they get ready to come to nursery class. Then the song will be sung as they play these preparations. For example, "This is the way we wash our face, this is the way we comb our hair, this is the way we brush our teeth, this is the way we put on our socks, this is the way we put on our clothes, this is the way we drink our milk," and so on. With a little encouragement the children will offer suggestions of their preparations.

ROUND WE GO

Let several children take hold of hands forming a circle. The teacher directs their movements by singing,

> "Round we go, round we go,
> All the children walking (running, skipping, hopping) so.
> Round we go the other way.
> Round we go the other way.
> All stand still and clap your hands,"

or an endless number of other variations. End this play by singing,

> "Round we go, round we go,
> All sit down on the floor,
> Close your eyes and take a rest."

Songs

LISTENING MUSIC

IN CHURCH

CRADLE SONG

Franz Schubert, Op. 98, No. 2
Slightly altered

Very slowly and gently

211

AWAY IN A MANGER

Carl Muller

A-way in a man-ger, no crib for a bed, The lit-tle Lord

Je-sus laid down His sweet head; The stars in the sky — looked

down where He lay, The lit-tle Lord Je-sus a-sleep on the hay.

WINTER FUN

Lois R. Donovan

V. Earle Copes

Slip - ping, slid-ing, tak-ing tum-bles, Laugh-ing, shar-ing, no one grum-bles. God, I think must sure-ly know What fun we have when there is snow.

SONGS FOR THE CHILDREN TO SING

CHURCH BELLS

From **Songs to Sing** by Edna M. Shaw. Adapted by permission of Edna M. Shaw.

FRIENDS AT CHURCH

Mary Edna Lloyd

Edna M. Shaw
Arranged by V. Earle Copes

LEAVES ARE FALLING

Mary Edna Lloyd

Arranged by V. Earle Copes

Leaves are fall - ing   down on the ground.
Red   and yel - low,   green leaves and brown.

Pret - ty   leaves fall down,   all   a - round.
Pret - ty   leaves fall down,   down, down, down.

LITTLE BABY JESUS

Ethel L. Smither

Natalie Robinson
Harmonized by J. Edward Moyer

Lit - tle Ba - by Je - sus slept so   qui - et - ly,

And his lov - ing mo - ther cared for him all the day.

Used by permission of Ethel L. Smither.

WHAT IS CHRISTMAS?

Esther Freivogel

Esther Freivogel
Arranged by V. Earle Copes

Christ-mas is Je-sus' birth-day. Christ-mas is Je — sus'

birth-day. That's why we're hap-py and that's why we're gay, For

Christ — mas is Je — sus' birth — day.

CHRISTMAS MORNING

Edna Shaw

Edna Shaw

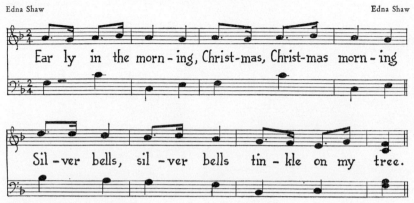

Ear ly in the morn-ing, Christ-mas, Christ-mas morn-ing

Sil-ver bells, sil-ver bells tin-kle on my tree.

Used by permission of the author.

THE SNOWMAN

Harmonized by V. Earle Copes

Snow-man, O! See him go! When the sun shines

on the snow, See him go! See him go!

From **Songs to Sing** by Edna Shaw. Used by permission of Edna M. Shaw.

THE REDBIRD

Maggie May Burrow

V. Earle Copes

The pret-ty red-bird with fea-thers so bright,
Comes to my win-dow morn-ing and night.
I watch to see him peck from the tray The
food I put out for him ev' - ry day.

MY FRIENDS

Maggie May Burrow

V. Earle Copes

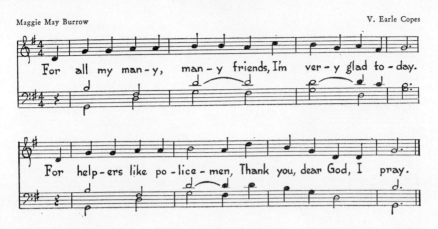

For all my man-y, man-y friends, I'm ver-y glad to-day.

For help-ers like po-lice-men, Thank you, dear God, I pray.

NEW CHICKS

Edna M. Shaw

Edna M. Shaw

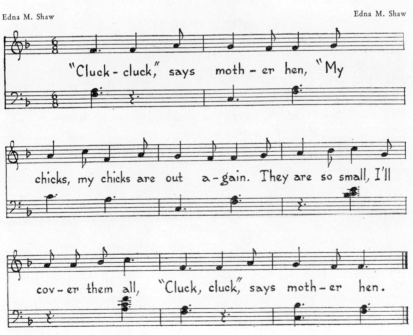

"Cluck-cluck," says moth-er hen, "My

chicks, my chicks are out a-gain. They are so small, I'll

cov-er them all, "Cluck, cluck," says moth-er hen.

Used by permission of Edna M. Shaw.

219

TEETER-TOTTER

A. S. Boesel
Arranged by V. Earle Copes

Here we go up and here we go down;

Tee — ter tot-ter to Lon — don town.

From **Sing and Sing Again,** by Ann Sterling Boesel.
Used by permission of Charles M. Boesel.

SPRING IS HERE

Laura Pendleton MacCarteney

Spring is here! I know, I know!

Ro — bin Red - breast told me so.

From **Songs for the Nursery School** by Laura Pendleton MacCarteney.
Copyright 1937 by The Willis Music Company. Used by permission.

TAKING TURNS

Mary Edna Lloyd

Melody by Natalie Robinson
Harmonized by J. Edward Moyer

Tak - ing turns in work and play Makes us hap - py ev - 'ry day. Tak - ing turns in work and play Makes us hap - py ev - 'ry day, Ev - 'ry day.

PITTER PATTER

Mary Edna Lloyd

Melody by Elsie L. Dwyer
Harmonized by J. Edward Moyer

Pit-ter, pat-ter, Hear the rain-drops Fall-ing to the ground.

Pit-ter, pat-ter, pit-ter, pat-ter, Fall-ing all a-round.

SING, O SING

Harmonized by V. Earle Copes

Sing, O-sing for it is spring.

Flow-ers bloom and rob-ins sing.

WHEN I'M VERY HAPPY

Mary Edna Lloyd

Edna M. Shaw

When I'm ver-y hap-py This is what I sing,

"Thank you, God, I thank you, Just for ev-'ry-thing."

HELPING MOTHER

Maggie May Burrow

V. Earle Copes

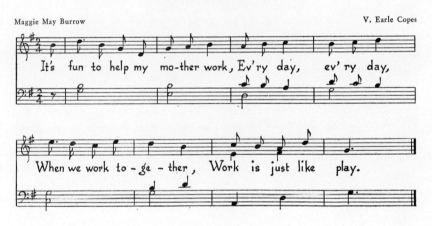

It's fun to help my mo-ther work, Ev'ry day, ev'ry day,

When we work to-ge-ther, Work is just like play.

223

GOD'S CARE

Edna M. Shaw

Edna M. Shaw
Arranged by V. Earle Copes

Birds fly in the sky so blue, God who made them cares for you. Lit - tle child - ren, thank Him too.

Used by permission of Edna M. Shaw.

CHURCH

Mary Edna Lloyd

Edna M. Shaw

Church, church, church. Thank you, God, for our church, for our church.

224

JESUS SAW THE FLOWERS

Maggie May Burrow

V. Earle Copes

Je-sus saw the flow-ers; He saw the song-birds too, He told of God who cared for them, He said, "And God loves you."

THE CHILDREN'S FRIEND

Jessie Eleanor Moore

H. H. Lemmel

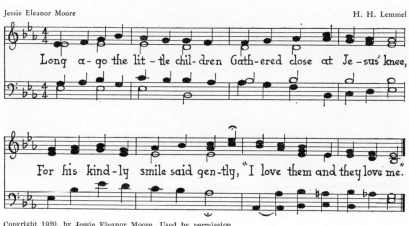

Long a-go the lit-tle chil-dren Gath-ered close at Je-sus' knee, For his kind-ly smile said gen-tly, "I love them and they love me."

GROWING

Helen H. Dietterich

Phil Dietterich

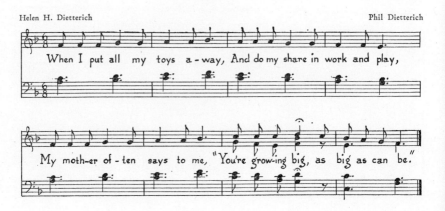

When I put all my toys a-way, And do my share in work and play,

My moth-er of-ten says to me, "You're grow-ing big, as big as can be."

ALL OF ME

Sadie K. Knight

Mary Lou Moody
Harmonized by V. Earle Copes

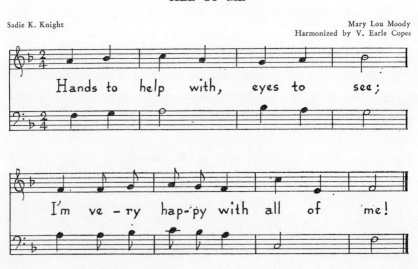

Hands to help with, eyes to see;

I'm ve - ry hap-py with all of me!

226

For the Teacher's Own Growth

GROWING PERSONS OF ANY AGE NEED TO BE ALERT, READY TO LEARN, eager to avail themselves of the best possible materials. Nursery class leaders are aware of the fact that great strides have been made in preschool education during recent years. Books are appearing. New pamphlets are available. Articles are printed in current magazines. Columns in newspapers suggest ways of learning from and living with nursery-age children.

Those working with three-year-olds need to know what has happened during the life span of each child and what is expected to happen within the next year or so as well as the to-be-expected development of the threes.

Watch *Child Guidance in Christian Living* for announcements and annotated lists of books.

Write to your conference board of education or to the Editorial Division, 201 Eighth Avenue South, Nashville, Tennessee for your annual copy of *Resources for Leaders of Children* leaflet No. 190-BE (free). Each year this publication carries a carefully selected list of books for workers with children as well as books for the children.

In addition to books that will help improve techniques of teaching, it is important that leaders have access to books for strengthening their own spiritual lives. Such books are included in *Child Guidance in Christian Living* and in *Resources for Leaders of Children*.

Still another means of growth is through the measuring of one's own teaching. This book has been planned with blank pages, "Notes." Use these pages for noting the books you have read to help you "grow" and the date of reading. If you use this textbook in a laboratory school situation, you may wish to make special notes of ideas gained.

Further use of the space will be in jotting down special "successes" or "failures" of the suggestions in this textbook. Which plans seemed to meet the needs of the children in an especially helpful way? Why? Which plans were failures? Why?

Each year that you teach in the nursery class should show improvement. You are not teaching a course as outlined by this textbook. You are teaching girls and boys. This textbook is merely a suggested guide as you discover needs of your own group and meet those needs in the best possible way to help supplement the work of parents in the home. Together, parents and teachers seek to nurture young children in Christian growth. May you find true joy in the Christian nurture of the three-year-olds in your church.

Notes

Notes

Notes

Notes

Notes

Notes

Notes

Notes

Notes

Notes

Notes

Notes

INFORMATION BLANK FOR NURSERY CHILD

Name _____

Name by which he is commonly called _____

Father's Name _____ Occupation _____

Mother's Name _____ Occupation _____

Address _____

Child's birth date _____

Has he been baptized? _____ In what church? _____

Church membership of Father _____ Mother _____

Name and relationship of other adults in his home _____

_____

What are his favorite play materials? _____

What does he say when he needs to be taken to the toilet? _____

Are there other children in his family? (List, giving ages) _____

_____

Names and ages of playmates _____

Does he attend nursery school? If so, which school? _____

Has he had any serious illnesses or operations? If so, what? Was he hos-

pitalized? _____

Does he say or hear prayers at home? (Describe) _____

_____

Does he have any habits or characteristics that you would like to have the

church school help you to strengthen or change? _____

_____